PAVAROTTI
LIFE WITH LUCIANO

PAVA
LIFE WITH LU

Adua

WEIDENFELD AND

ROTTI
CIANO

Pavarotti
WITH *Wendy Dallas*

SPECIAL PHOTOGRAPHY BY
*Judith Kovacs, Robin Matthews
and Mirella Ricciardi*

NICOLSON · LONDON

Contents

'Opera is his
passion, and, since
he is a man who
needs to share his joys in life with other people,
he has committed himself throughout his career
to making it as accessible to everyone as
it was to him when he was young.'

1   An Operatic Inheritance

When Luciano stands in the spotlight at the end of a solo concert, with a hundred thousand people still crying out for more, it is hard to comprehend that this is only a tiny fraction of his audience and that live television and radio broadcasts will be followed up by video, cassette and disc recordings to take his voice to millions more around the world. In 1961, when I married him and his career was just beginning, fame beyond the narrow limits of the operatic world was almost inconceivable for anyone in his profession, and his highest ambition was one day to play the tenor leads in international productions, but his individual blend of qualities and talent has worked a particularly potent sort of alchemy. The fact that he has succeeded in breaking all the rules, and achieved infinitely more than he aspired to, is due in no small part to his personality.

Almost everyone knows that Luciano

Pavarotti is a big, warm-hearted Italian singer, that he loves to eat and is crazy about football, and perhaps, since the Italia '90 World Cup, they also know him as the man who took Puccini's 'Nessun dorma' to number one in the charts. To understand his success, and what it is about his voice that stops people in their tracks, I believe you need to appreciate how clearly he reflects his origins and to know the man himself a little better. I am not attempting here to write the story of his life, only to fill in some of the missing pieces in the picture so that his name conjures up an image not just of a great, exuberant Italian tenor but of a man who is passionately committed to everything he does, who is disciplined in his working life and childishly irrepressible in

At Covent Garden in 1984 Luciano appeared in Verdi's Aida *with Katia Ricciarelli, Stefania Toczyska and Ingvar Wixell.*

Luciano owes his love of music, the force that motivates his life, to an operatic tradition that is firmly rooted in the region where he was born.

Luciano in the role of the Egyptian General, Radames, in the Covent Garden production of Aida, *1984.*

his capacity for having fun, who is endearingly generous and impossibly demanding, who has close family relationships, impulsive shopping sprees, an exaggerated interest in his health, and a love of people that he communicates to his fans and to everyone he meets.

When we were children we had just enough to live on and life was very simple; now we have a great deal more

and it is extraordinarily complicated, but the changes did not happen overnight, we have had time to adjust, and our peasant background, which helped to make Luciano as natural and unpretentious as he is, has kept our feet fairly firmly on the ground. For all Italians the most binding attachments, aside from the family, are to the town or village in which we are brought up, and local

affiliations and traditions exert such a powerful hold on us that we are influenced by them all our lives. *Campanilismo*, pride in one's home town, is a peculiarly Italian concept, and has the effect of consolidating influences which in other countries tend to be more disparate. We are inseparable from our origins, and Luciano's sense of belonging to Modena, the small northern Italian city where

he was born, is very strong (even the name Pavarotti derives from a *modenese* dialect word) because as well as being his home base it is where all his deepest loyalties lie.

In a wider sense he is rooted in Emilia Romagna, a region famous for its music and above all its food. It stretches across the south-eastern quarter of the vast low-lying plain of the Po Valley, its flat

A scene from the second act of Verdi's Un Ballo in Maschera *at the Grand Theatre, Geneva, 30 January 1984, with mezzosoprano Mignon Dunn in the role of Ulrica.*

horizons pierced by the ancient towers of Parma, Modena, Bologna, Ferrara and Ravenna. Intersected throughout its length and breadth by tributaries of the Po, it is a land of well-watered vineyards, orchards and wheat fields, its outlines softened by the humidity of the summer heat and by the fog that shrouds the winter landscape and drifts among the poplar trees along the river banks. We have always lived on the edge of town, with farmland all around us, and Luciano has a deep affinity with the country. He dreams of farming our own few acres when he has more time, growing grain and grapes and fruit trees; if he could make his own pasta and wine he would have the best things in life on his doorstep.

He is famous for his love of food, and has done his conspicuous best to advertise our great regional cuisine, whose staple ingredients – dairy products, pork and pasta – are all produced here (*par-*

migiano, or parmesan cheese, and a particularly delicious prosciutto both come from the Parma area), together with strawberries, cherries, peaches, apples, pears and Lambrusco wine. Most *emiliani* (the people of our area) will happily spend hours of every day in lively discussion of the finer points of a *cotechino* (a much respected local sausage), preparing home-made tagliatelle, minestrone or *bol-*

ABOVE *In discussion with Herbert von Karajan, silhouetted against the set of* Tosca *at the Festspielhaus, Salzburg, March 1989.*
LEFT *Ponchielli's* La Gioconda *at the Verona Arena, July 1980, with Luciano in the role of Enzo Grimaldo.*

lito misto (a dish of mixed boiled meats) and sitting down with the family to relish the results of their labours. Luciano, like most Italians, is sociable by nature and loves to spend an evening surrounded by friends *con le gambe sotto il tavolo* – with their legs under the table – because it provides not just an excuse for eating and drinking but an opportunity to talk, relax and enjoy each other's company.

ABOVE *On 14 August 1985 Luciano gave his first solo recital in his home town of Modena, his voice ringing round the arcades of the Piazza Grande and across the square to the Romanesque cathedral. His close family and friends were there, together with an enormous gathering of the local population.*

BELOW *A scene from Puccini's* La Bohème, *Peking, 1986, with Kalen Esperian as Mimi, Madelyn Renee (right) as Musetta and Luciano as Rodolfo. Bohème has a special significance for Luciano because it is the opera in which he made his début on the opera stage.*

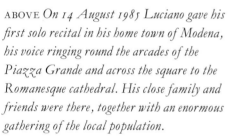

Emiliani are famous for their size and their appetites; typically the men are strong and broad-chested, and Luciano would be the first to endorse the theory that all this robust, wholesome food produces great singers. It is certainly true that you need a muscular chest to produce a big sound and that our region has proved to be fertile ground for opera singers. Vocal music is almost as important as food to *emiliani*, and its influence permeated every layer of the society in which Luciano was brought up. When opera was invented in the late sixteenth century – by an Italian tenor working in Florence – it rapidly became an entertainment exclusively for the rich, and has remained so in many other countries, but in Italy, and especially in Emilia Romagna, private and public subsidies have brought it within the reach of almost

LEFT *The Neopolitans gave Luciano a spectacular reception when he appeared, with Leone Magiera at the piano, in a recital at the Teatro San Carlo in May 1987. The banner reads 'Come back Pavarotti, we are waiting for you'.*
BELOW *A solo recital at the Grosser Musikvereinsaal in Vienna, 4 June 1989.*

everyone. Although it is struggling to survive, opera has never become elitist here; it belongs to all of us, and before the days of modern farm machinery, when the hay was still cut with a scythe, it was common to hear peasant farmers singing arias from *Rigoletto* and *Un Ballo in Maschera* as they worked in the fields.

Even in recent years this strong operatic tradition has produced some great singers: Gianni Raimondi and Ruggero Raimondi, both from Bologna, Carlo Bergonzi from Parma and our contemporary and lifelong friend Mirella Freni from Modena among them. And it is not just the professionals who are experts on technique and the art of *bel canto* – beautiful tone, good phrasing and clear enunciation – everyone is. When Luciano was young, his father, Fernando, sang in the chorus of the Modena opera

A talent for singing runs in the Pavarotti family: Luciano inherited his musical gifts from his father, Fernando, and he in turn from his mother. Even now, at the age of eighty, Fernando has a fine strong tenor voice and sings every day. He and Luciano have performed many times together, and in October 1989 they sang with the Corale Rossini in a concert at the Municipio, Modena.

house and in the church and cathedral choirs, and Luciano insists that his father's voice was more beautiful than his own. A number of people had offered to pay for Fernando to study because he could never have found the money himself, but whenever he sang the solo at vespers at the little local church of San Geminiano he suffered such terrible stage fright that it was apparent a career as an opera singer was more than his nerves could stand. He has always been passionate about vocal music, and when Luciano was a boy Fernando used to bring home gramophone records of all the great tenors of the time – Caruso, Gigli, Schipa and Martinelli. So Luciano was steeped in opera from birth, and perhaps it was natural that he would try to emulate the voices that he heard around him.

The beauty of his individual sound is a gift, but he has devoted most of his life to training his voice, and from the day he began studying he was totally committed to perfecting it. His first teacher, Arrigo Pola, has said that it was his dedication to learning coupled with quickness of mind that was his most important attribute after the voice itself, and his technique is now generally considered, by critics and musicians alike, to be faultless.

Among the aspects of his singing that are always praised is his clean articulation, on which he worked long and hard with Pola; not only does it make the libretto easier to understand but it enhances both the relationship of the words to the music and the beauty of the language itself. Another is his smooth legato line and perfect phrasing; he

knows exactly when to come in a fraction before or after the beat or sustain a note a little longer than usual in order to heighten the drama or the tenderness of a musical phrase, not an easy thing to learn but to Luciano it comes naturally. His accompanist for many years, John Wustman, has said that he is 'super musical' with an 'instinctive overall comprehension of the composer's intentions and he has no trouble getting these qualities into the music he sings'. Luciano has sometimes been criticized because he is not as fine an actor as some of his colleagues, and he would be the first to admit that he is no Laurence Olivier, but he does believe that as a singer he should be able to express every human emotion through his voice. The success of his recordings no doubt owes a good deal to his ability to act through his singing, concentrating everything he has on expressing the mood of the music, which he knows is the only way to move people.

He regards his voice almost as a separate entity, as if it has a life of its own. It has good days and bad like the rest of us, but it is capable, when in good form, of anything he asks of it. His love of opera, like his appetite and openness, belongs to his roots in Modena, and above all he wants to use his voice to make the music that he grew up with something that everyone can share.

Luciano went to his first opera at the age of twelve, and ever since then he has been convinced that people who queue for hours to sit in the cheapest seats are more likely to be moved by what they hear than those who pay a fortune to sit 'down in the suits', as he puts it, who sometimes seem impervious to the beauty of the music. Opera is his passion, the force that motivates his life, and, since he is a man who needs to share his joys with other people, he has committed himself throughout his career to making it as accessible to everyone as it was to him when he was young.

ABOVE *A gala concert was held to mark the twenty-fifth anniversary of the founding of the Metropolitan Opera, New York, on 23 September 1991, the first night of the new season. Placido Domingo and Luciano, in the roles of Marcello and Rodolfo, performed a piece from* La Bohème.

LEFT *Raina Kabaivanska in the title role and Luciano as the painter, Mario Cavaradossi, in a production of Puccini's* Tosca *at the Opera di Roma, December 1990.*

Luciano in one of his favourite roles, Nemorino, in Donizetti's L'Elisir d'Amore, *which he performed at the Royal Opera House, Covent Garden, in 1990 with Daniela Mazzucato as Adina.*

2
Beginnings

'*He was charismatic and confident, the one his friends seemed automatically to look to as the leader of the pack, and during the evening passeggiata, when the population of Modena turns out to stroll around the Piazza Grande and along the arcaded streets, he always stood out from the crowd.*'

It was a hot Sunday afternoon in September 1953 when we met. Luciano was seventeen and I was a year younger. Having, like most young Italians, left Scuola Media (the equivalent of secondary school) at the age of fourteen, we were both now attending the local Istituto Magistrale, though in different classes, taking a four-year diploma course that would qualify us to teach in elementary school. Luciano was still undecided about his future career, but he was anxious to have something to fall back on if all else failed.

We had been invited independently to a birthday party given by a fellow student, a boy whom I found *antipatico*, and I had tried to find an excuse to refuse the invitation, but a friend of mine persuaded me to go. Luciano was eye-catching, *un bel ragazzone*. He says he loved the red-and-white check dress I was wearing – it reminded him of the tablecloths in a trattoria – and he came over as soon as he saw me. He was lively and flirtatious and asked me to the cinema the following week. I agreed on condition that my cousin and another friend came too, a proviso which he reluctantly accepted, though later I discovered he had tried to dissuade them from coming.

Luciano (centre) at the age of fifteen, summer 1951, at Pesaro on the Adriatic coast with two bolognese friends, Gianni Piazzi (left) and Pierfrancesco Senesi (right). We spent an evening reminiscing with them recently when they brought their wives to dinner at our house in Modena.

We met again soon afterwards at another party at the house of a mutual friend, where the guests were induced to attempt a traditional song or a well-known aria from Italian opera. Luciano, the only one with any real talent for singing, sang 'Rondine al nido' (a beautiful song which has for many years now formed part of his concert repertoire), but in those days I had no real feeling for serious music – I much preferred American songs like 'Summertime' which was popular then – and I confess that his singing made little impression. My own voice has always been a husky, rather tuneless baritone, and when it came to my turn I sang a piece from *Rigoletto* so horribly badly that Luciano decided I needed his help and protection.

We began to see each other regularly after that, both in and out of school. He was charismatic and confident, the one his friends seemed automatically to look to as the leader of the pack, and during the evening *passeggiata*, when the population of Modena turns out rain or shine to stroll around the Piazza Grande and along the arcaded streets, he always stood out from the crowd. He and some of the boys he knew liked to congregate on the corner outside the Café Molinari and watch the girls go by, but in spite of his obvious appeal Luciano was never the typical Italian lover; he was stable, serious-minded and mature for his age – *molto uomo* – very much a man. We soon realized that we wanted our relationship to be more than just a casual flirtation, and in June 1954 we became engaged. At that time young people frequently became *fidanzati* simply to spend time alone together, which would otherwise not have been proper, but in our case the engagement was made to last – for over seven years as it turned out. In the first few months, however, it was punctuated by seemingly irreconcilable rows and separations at least three times a week. Storms blew up out of petty disagree-ments almost every time we met, and once, after an even more final and irreparable rift than usual, we split up for a year. Then we tried again, and decided that this time we would stay together.

Modena in the 1950s was not the rich city it has since become. Much of the industry that had grown up around its medieval core before the war had been destroyed by bombing, and like every-where else in Europe it was now strug-gling to put its life back together again. It was during the early '50s that the first signs of the economic boom which was to transform northern Italy within two decades gradually began to appear. But Modena was still a quiet place; people slept with their front doors open, there was no drug problem, and we were a great deal more carefree than the younger generation is today. We had none of their concerns about philosoph-ical issues – ours were more fundamental and immediate because the war had made the future so uncertain – and there were not the same opportunities for spending money even if we had had it. At the weekends Luciano and I used to join up with friends and go dancing, usually at the Eden café in the town, which held tea dances for students on Saturday after-noons, or sometimes we went to the cinema, a local skating rink, a volleyball or football match. In the summer we went for walks along the Secchia, the river that runs through Modena's wes-tern reaches on its way north to join the Po; if we could borrow bicycles we took a picnic and went off for the day.

One Sunday we persuaded an uncle of Luciano's to lend us his much-prized motor scooter so that we could visit my eldest sister, Loredana, who lived with her husband at Riva on Lake Garda, a three-hour ride away to the north. We left at five in the morning, with the midsummer sun just beginning to rise over the plain that stretches away from Modena as far as the foothills of the

Dolomites. Once we were well away from the town Luciano urged me to sit in front and try my hand at steering. '*Dai, provaci*' – come on, try it – he said. I was reluctant but he persisted, and his powers of persuasion were as effective then as they are now. There was a bend in the road, and as we neared it he told me to begin swinging round to follow the curve. I called back, telling him not to worry, it was a wide bend, and he was still shouting out '*Curva! Curva! Curva!*' when we hit a signpost straight ahead and shot over the handlebars, landing in a field with the scooter on top of us. Luckily we were on the edge of a village and there was a chemist nearby where we could patch ourselves up, but it was still only half-past six and while we waited for it to open we went into a little church and thanked the good Lord for saving our lives. We then sent a telegram to my sister and spent the rest of the day sitting on a bench in a public garden while a local mechanic fixed the engine. When we arrived home we put all our savings together to have the rest of the scooter repaired.

In those days seats in the *loggione* (the gods) at the Teatro Comunale in Modena cost very little more than a cinema ticket, and we went to all the new operatic productions. Luciano, like his father, regularly sang in choral works both at the opera house and the cathedral, and it was with the opera choir, the Corale Rossini, that he and Fernando went to Britain for the first time, in July 1955, to compete in the Royal National Eisteddfod at Llangollen in Wales. During the week they were to be away Luciano, then nineteen, was due to take his final exams before leaving the Istituto Magistrale, and was so determined not to miss the trip that he asked for permission from the board of examiners to sit them a few days early. It meant taking all his diploma papers in the space of three days, and the rush, combined with anticipation of the excitement ahead, produced predictably mediocre results. The Corale Rossini did a great deal better. They were competing against twenty-two choirs from countries all over the world, and their choirmaster, Livio Borri, had told them beforehand that he would be delighted if they made it into the last ten; by the time the last three competitors were announced and they had still not been eliminated he had reached such a state of euphoria that he passed out – or so the story goes – and had to be rapidly revived with brandy in order to collect the first prize.

BELOW *Luciano at a few months old. His mother, Adele, has never forgotten the words of the doctor as her new-born son lay screaming in her arms:* 'Mamma mia, che acuti!' – '. . . what high notes!'

RIGHT *Luciano, aged five, and his baby sister, Gabriella, with their Aunt Marta in the garden of the Modena apartment block where both the children were born. Sixteen other families shared the building, and as the only boy in the neighbourhood Luciano enjoyed the attentation of them all.*

OPPOSITE *Dressed for his confirmation.*

Even at the age of five Luciano loved to sing, entertaining the neighbours – most of them relations or close friends – with recitals in the courtyard of the apartment block in which his family lived on the outskirts of the town. He used to set up a little child's chair by the fountain and accompany himself on a toy mandolin given to him by his parents, and although he often says the neighbours used to yell at him to stop, I have also heard it said that he was thrown sweets and nuts as a reward. People tell me he was a beguiling little boy, with a desire to please which everyone found irresistible.

Born on 12 October 1935, Luciano was the first child and only son of Fernando and Adele Pavarotti. His pa-

rents had lived in Modena all their lives, and the small city and its surroundings formed the background to a world to which they belonged. Fernando was one of eight children, Adele one of five, and they both had brothers and sisters living close by with children of their own. They were as united as most Italian families of the time and they knew they could depend on each other for help whenever they needed it. Both of Luciano's parents went out to work, his father in a local bakery, his mother in a cigar factory, and – unlike many others who had survived the war but had no earnings to support them in peacetime – the family never went hungry; they lived modestly but they were content with what comforts they had. Luciano was the first boy to have been born in the immediate area for ten years, and he was treated as special not just by his female relations but by all the women in the neighbourhood.

To his mother's mother, Nonna Giulia, he was more than just a favourite grandchild: her own youngest daughter, Lucia, after whom he was named, had died at the age of twelve the year before he was born, and in many respects he replaced the little girl in his grandmother's heart. Since his parents were at work all day it was largely Nonna Giulia who brought him up, and the bond that formed between them was very strong. She was a woman of great character, for whom the family was all-important, prepared philosophically to put up with almost anything in order to keep it together; she turned a blind eye to her husband's philandering, letting him please himself when he was out of the house – and he pleased himself a good deal – but insisting that within their own four walls she had the last word. She had received no formal education but she had the instinctive wisdom of many of the women of Emilia Romagna. Luciano adored her and she would do anything in the world for him, always standing up for

ABOVE *Nine-year-old Luciano with
Gabriella, five. Their childhood was happy
and secure, and even evacuation, to escape the
worst of the bombing during the war, held its
compensations. The Pavarotti family rented
a room from a farmer in the small village of
Gargallo, near Carpi, and Luciano spent his
days helping in the fields, an experience which
gave him a love of animals and the country
which has never left him.*

RIGHT *On holiday at Santa Margherita in
Liguria, August 1951: Luciano with his
mother and sister.*

OPPOSITE *This photograph of me posing on
the beach was taken at Cattolica, near
Rimini, in September 1955, in the second
year of our engagement.*

him when he got into arguments and allowing him to be right. She made his favourite minestrone as often as he wanted it and, within their limited resources, gave him everything she could.

As a child he had a great deal of freedom and spent most of his time playing football, hunting frogs in the neighbouring woods, and singing. By the time he was nine or ten he was trying out a few arias on the neighbours – 'La donna è mobile' from *Rigoletto* was his speciality – and one or two people began to take his voice more seriously. His musical talent was a source of pride and delight to his father, but Fernando was reluctant to encourage him when later on Luciano considered taking up singing professionally; he had seen so many people waste years of their lives studying to become singers and finish up with nothing, and he did not want to see this happen to his son. In the Pavarotti

Only if we stayed with relatives could we spend a night away from home in the years before we married, but on Sundays in the summer we occasionally managed a day trip to the coast.

household there were long discussions around the table as to which path Luciano should follow when he left the Istituto Magistrale. He was a good athlete and one possible option was to train as a sports instructor, but this would have meant leaving Modena which he was loath to do; another was to take a degree course at university, which would have equipped him to teach in secondary school; a third was to study singing and try to get established as a professional. His mother, who has always had an excellent ear for music and instinctively good judgement of vocal technique, decided it should be singing; when he sang his voice moved her, she said. It was agreed that his parents would continue to support him at home until he was thirty, and if he had had no real success by then he would abandon all thoughts of an operatic career and find something else to do with his life.

ABOVE *The Lepanto team – 1952 champions of the province of Modena – in which Luciano (back row, extreme right) played centre forward. The photograph, dated 24 April 1952, is dedicated to him by their manager:* 'A Luciano Pavarotti, che ha portato il suo "peso" per la nostra bella vittoria' – *'To Luciano Pavarotti, who lent his "weight" to our great victory.'*

OPPOSITE ABOVE *The Corale Rossini, winners of the choral competition at the Royal National Eisteddfod in Wales, 1955. The choirmaster, Livio Borri, can be seen holding up the first prize; below him to the left is Luciano and to the right, with a large expanse of shirt front, is Fernando.*

OPPOSITE BELOW *Arrigo Pola in 1957 with pupils Bindo Verrini (left) and Luciano. The dedication reads:* 'Caro Luciano, ascoltami e arriverai certamente!!! Studia e sii tenace! Sinceramente Arrigo Pola' – *'Dear Luciano, listen to me and you will undoubtedly make it!!! Study and be determined! . . .'*

His first teacher was a highly regarded professional tenor living in Modena, Maestro Arrigo Pola, who was not only struck by the quality of Luciano's voice but recognized in him instantly the makings of a *primo tenore*, a leading tenor. Knowing the family's financial situation, he agreed to give him free lessons. Luciano began his studies with him in 1955, working relentlessly for the first six months on exercises to stretch the facial muscles and produce clear, rounded vowel sounds. He has a capacity to throw himself into almost anything he does, and he became fascinated by the technicalities of singing. The endlessly repeated scales – the solfeggio – and the breathing exercises and vocal routines which many singers find boring he enjoyed, and it intrigued him to discover the way his voice responded to different techniques.

While he studied with Maestro Pola Luciano took a part-time job in the local elementary school where I worked myself; at various times he taught music, religion, gymnastics and sport, and although he loved sport he found the children impossible to discipline and exhausting to teach. Before long he was offered a more congenial occupation and one for which, as it turned out, he had a remarkable talent. An insurance company which had an arrangement with the school took him on as a salesman, and the pupils' families provided him with a ready-made clientele to whom he was already a familiar figure. His natural charm and persuasiveness did the rest and soon he was earning good wages. Indeed he became so useful to the company that his boss, who had never taken seriously his wish to become a singer, offered him the management of a branch office in a nearby town. As a singer, he used to say, you will undoubtedly die of starvation while in insurance '*il pane è sicuro*' – you will have bread for life.

In 1956 Arrigo Pola left Modena to take up a post in Japan, handing Luciano over to the best teacher he knew in Italy, Ettore Campogalliani of Mantua. Luciano continued his studies with his new maestro, making the hour's journey by train twice a week to his lessons, and working hard to improve his range and technique and develop his instinctive talent for musical phrasing. He had become so good at selling insurance that his job was beginning to put a strain on his voice, and the following year he decided to give it up and devote himself with even greater commitment to singing. Campogalliani was a wonderful teacher and offered him every encouragement, but when another two years had passed and Luciano had still had no offers of work, disillusionment began to set in. So far his only commission had been a request from a local boy for help in courting his girlfriend; like Don Giovanni or Cyrano de Bergerac, Luciano ser-

enaded her with an aria while his friend, Luciano Ghelfi (whom we have known all our lives), stood under her window pretending it was him.

Most of our friends were settling into good careers and could afford to get married, and, although I was in no hurry to do so because I was well aware of how restricted one's life becomes when children are part of it, Luciano was depressed at his lack of progress. By now it was nearly six years since his first lessons with Pola, and to persevere for so long re-

quired great conviction. He was still determined it was to be *primo tenore* or nothing, and if he could not be in the front rank he would give up singing completely, resign from the Modena choirs and never set foot in an opera house again. When in 1960 he developed a small polyp in his throat and as a result gave a poor performance at a recital in Ferrara, he was almost ready to admit defeat. He was booked for one more concert, at Salsomaggiore Terme near Parma, two weeks later; in the interim he

rested his vocal cords, and miraculously he sang better on the night than he had ever sung in his life. Psychologically this was the turning point, and when he continued to do well in recitals in local towns he began to feel at last that he might make it.

Early in 1961, at the age of twenty-five, he entered the international Achille Peri competition for young singers. The first prize was the role of Rodolfo in Puccini's *La Bohème* in a production directed by the great *ferrarese* soprano

The opera bill for the 1961 production of La Bohème *at the Teatro Municipale, Reggio Emilia, in which Luciano played the part of Rodolfo, the first prize in the international Achille Peri competition. Fernando Pavarotti played a supporting role.*

Mafalda Favero, to be staged at the Teatro Municipale in Reggio Emilia a few weeks later, on 29 April. To our enormous elation and joy, he won. Rodolfo is a wonderful role for a lyric tenor and perfect for Luciano's voice. He threw himself into rehearsals with all his old enthusiasm, and on the night, under the baton of Maestro Molinari-Pradelli, he had a triumph. He also had a stroke of luck because in the audience was an important agent from Milan, an ex-tenor called Alessandro Ziliani, who was there more out of curiosity than anything else, to hear the bass Dmitri Nabokov, son of the writer whose book *Lolita* was then on everyone's lips. He found his attention taken instead by Luciano, and for the next few years devoted himself to helping him get established.

Things were looking good and we felt that at last we could afford to take the next step: we fixed the date for our wedding. Luciano spent much of the summer studying new roles, the Duke of Mantua in *Rigoletto* and Alfredo in *La Traviata*, and on 14 September 1961 he made his début as a professional singer in *La Bohème* at the Teatro Comunale del Giglio in Lucca. It went well, and – which was almost equally important at the time – he was paid 60,000 lire (equivalent in those days to about £35) for two performances. A fortnight later, on 30 September 1961, we were married, in the church of San Faustino in Modena.

We married in September 1961, the month of Luciano's début on the opera stage. In the seven years of our engagement I had never agonized over the economics of our future together – Luciano has always had what it takes to survive, and I knew that we could both have made a living – but he had been anxious to get a foothold on the opera ladder before we went ahead with the wedding. Winning the Achille Peri award gave him the start that he needed.

ABOVE *Outside the church of San Faustino, Modena.*

RIGHT *A family group: to Luciano's left is his mother, Adele; to my right is my father, Guido Veroni.*

ABOVE *Luciano and I with Fernando and Adele Pavarotti and Luciano's paternal grandfather, Vittorio Pavarotti, at the reception in a local restaurant.*

After the wedding we set off in an ancient little Fiat — Luciano's pride and joy — on a two-week honeymoon to Florence and the Italian Riviera.

3 Primo Tenore

'He had to wait five years to make up for the disappointment of his début at the Met, but when he returned with Joan Sutherland in 1972, in Covent Garden's production of La Fille du Régiment, he had the sort of history-making triumph that he had longed for.'

On 22 September 1961, the day after Luciano's last performance of *La Bohème* in Lucca, he had an audition, arranged by Ziliani, for the role of the Duke of Mantua in *Rigoletto* at Palermo's famous Teatro Massimo. The conductor was the great Maestro Tullio Serafin, then eighty-three years of age and revered by everyone in the opera world. Luciano was extremely nervous. The audition was in Rome at four in the afternoon and, having arrived two hours early, he walked about in a state of mounting tension until the appointed hour. At last he was ushered in. Serafin was a man of few words and, having greeted him briefly, asked the maid, Rosina, to bring Luciano a glass of water, dismissing his assurances that he had already had a drink at a local bar: 'You may not be thirsty now, but I assure you that you will be later.' He sat down at the piano and turned to page one of the score. Luciano had expected simply to be asked to sing 'La donna è mobile' or some other aria, but Serafin intended to go through the entire opera and by the end of the second act Luciano was gasping for a drink of water. Serafin smiled for the first time and indicated the glass. It became apparent in the course of the last act, although he said nothing, that Serafin liked what he was hearing, and at the end he merely said, 'Now when you come to Palermo I want you to sing "Bella figlia dell'amore" with exaggeration, the way Caruso did...'. Luciano understood then that he had the part, and he came

One of Luciano's first publicity portraits taken at a photographic studio in Modena, September 1961.

back to Modena that night looking as if he had won the national lottery.

This was his first real step on the ladder, but when he set off for Palermo in February of the following year it was also our first long separation. I had given up my teaching job a few months before and was working in the offices of the Agricultural Association in Modena; I could not take time off to go with him and I was in any case by then expecting our first child. We both cried when we said goodbye at the station; he was to be away for five weeks and it felt as if we would never see each other again.

Our first daughter, Lorenza, was born just over a year after we married, on 26 October 1962. It was the last night of *Rigoletto* at Rovigo, a town to the northeast of Modena, with Luciano playing the Duke. As his father left to see the evening's performance my labour pains began, but I told Fernando not to mention this to Luciano before the curtain went up because I was concerned that nothing should distract him from his

ABOVE LEFT *In costume as the Duke of Mantua in Verdi's* Rigoletto, *with Maestro Tullio Serafin, backstage at the Teatro Massimo, Palermo, January 1962.* ABOVE RIGHT *Luciano and I on a trip to Trieste, Spring 1962.*

singing. Afterwards one of the cast insisted they had a party to celebrate the end of the run, and Luciano was persuaded to go. Thinking he was still to keep silent, Fernando kept my news to himself; the party went on until the early hours and, on this one occasion, Luciano decided to come home the following day. As soon as he arrived back at Modena station he telephoned our flat, and since there was no reply he rang his sister, Gabriella, who explained that I was in hospital and had had a baby girl. He was upset to have missed the birth and horrified to learn from her that I had been haemorrhaging badly and for a while the doctors had not known if I would live or die. By the time he came to see me I was out of danger and all was well, but he had wanted the first child to be a boy and could not hide his disappointment at the arrival of a daughter.

When we married we had moved into a little two-room apartment that my father had rented for us across the hall from his own (my mother had died when

ABOVE *My sister Giovanna (left) and I were both pregnant, she with her second child, I with my first, when we went on holiday with her family to Viserba, near Rimini, in August 1962. On the right is Luciano and in the foreground Giovanna's son Marco.*
ABOVE RIGHT *Five generations of the Pavarotti family: Luciano with (left to right) his grandmother, Nonna Giulia, his great grandmother, Bisnonna Cristina, and his mother, Adele, holding our first child, Lorenza.*

When we first married we lived in a rented apartment, across the hall from my father, on the top floor of this small block on the outskirts of Modena.

I was six). My sister Giovanna, her husband and baby lived there with him, and until the wedding I had done so too. I continued to work at the Agricultural Association, and we scraped by on my small salary until Luciano began earning regular fees. In those early days I used to travel with him as often as I could, leaving Lorenza with my sister.

There were many more great tenors on the opera circuit then than there are now – Franco Corelli, Giuseppe di Stefano, Mario del Monaco, Gianni Raimondi, Carlo Bergonzi and several others among them – and for the first year or two Luciano had only a sprinkling of engagements in provincial theatres up and down the country. Gradually, because foreign opera houses were more businesslike than our own, planning their productions much further ahead, he began to get more bookings around Europe than at home. He was very conscious of being dependent on me financially during the first two or three years of our marriage, and when he had a windfall he made the

It was a struggle to break into a world in which so many great tenors were established, and Luciano worked hard to build up a repertoire and become known on the international opera network.

most of it. I remember coming back from the office one evening in January 1963, Luciano having been away for a few weeks touring in Holland in *Lucia di Lammermoor*, to find our bedroom covered in banknotes. The Italian opera company had been short of money, and instead of paying the singers weekly they had paid them in cash at the end of the run. In those days 10,000-lire notes were as big as posters, and he had papered the walls with them and all the furniture too – the dressing-table, the wardrobe, the bed, everything.

By 1963 his repertoire consisted of *La Bohème*, *Madama Butterfly*, *Rigoletto*, *La Traviata* and *Lucia di Lammermoor*, and he was in *Rigoletto* at the Gaiety Theatre in Dublin in May 1963 when he was spotted by Joan Ingpen, then casting director at the Royal Opera House, Covent Garden, who was scouting for new talent. Four months later, when Giuseppe di Stefano fell ill, Luciano was called on to step into the role of Rodolfo in Covent Garden's *Bohème*. The morning after his début an article appeared in the London *Times* headed 'Discovery of great new Italian tenor'. He spoke almost no English in those days but everyone took to him at Covent Garden because he was attractive and fun, and because he had stepped into the breach at the last minute.

One weekend while he was in that first London *Bohème* he and some other friends were invited by Enid Blech, then assistant to Georg Solti (who was music director at Covent Garden), to her cottage at Alfriston in East Sussex. She was a delightful and remarkable woman who spoke seven languages and flew her own plane, and over the years she was to

become a very dear friend. Luciano went out riding on the Sunday afternoon and when he got back to the house, aching in every muscle and looking forward to a soak in a long relaxing bath, he found everyone in a panic: 'Quick, quick, you must get to the station', they urged him; 'di Stefano has cancelled Sunday Night at the London Palladium and they want you to replace him.' Luciano thought longingly of the bath, but they insisted: 'You don't understand,' they said, 'it's the biggest television show in England; everybody watches it. You have to go.' Perhaps it was the charge of adrenalin that made him sing brilliantly that night, but the audience, both in the theatre and at home, was rapturously enthusiastic; hardly any of them had ever heard of him before and that one appearance made him known to more people in Britain than he could have reached in a lifetime on the opera stage.

The offer of the role of Idamante in Glyndebourne's 1964 production of *Idomeneo* was a spin-off from his Covent Garden success. By this time I was pregnant with our second child so my father went with Luciano to England in my place, and they rented a cottage in East Sussex which belonged to a friend of Enid Blech. It was the first time Luciano had tackled Mozart and *Idomeneo*

ABOVE *Luciano as Pinkerton in* Madama Butterfly, *Palermo, February 1964.*
OPPOSITE *With Gundula Janowitz in a Glyndebourne Festival production of* Idomeneo, *May 1964. George Christie of Glyndebourne saw a dimension in Luciano that set him apart from other singers; he referred to him as 'one of nature's virtues'.*

La Traviata at the Royal Opera House, Covent Garden, March 1965, with Renata Scotto as Violetta and Luciano as Alfredo.

was a daunting prospect. Having trained with provincial Italian opera companies, he found Glyndebourne's approach alarmingly serious at first, but he loved the sense of commitment that he felt all around him, and learned a lot about stagecraft and about English discipline and professionalism. He never travels between performances once he has begun an engagement, and I have never asked him to do anything that might interfere with his work, but I was sad not to have him with me when our second daughter, Cristina, was born on 4 August 1964, two weeks before he came home.

It was Joan Ingpen who that same year introduced Luciano to Joan Sutherland and her husband Richard Bonynge, an encounter which was to lead to a long-term collaboration and friendship that influenced the whole course of his career. At nearly six feet (1.82 metres), he is taller than most of his colleagues, and his height as well as his voice made him the perfect partner for Joan; almost immediately she and Richard booked him to join them on a tour of Australia in 1965. In the meantime Joan was delighted to be able to persuade the Miami Opera House management to accept him as a replacement when the Italian tenor Renato Cioni cancelled his engagement in *Lucia di Lammermoor*, which he was to have performed with her in February 1965. The Miami audience responded with great warmth to Luciano, and this appearance was a vital help to him in getting established in the United States.

He returned twice to Covent Garden in 1965, to appear in *La Traviata* and *La Sonnambula*, and it was these two operas, together with *Lucia di Lammermoor*, that he sang with Joan Sutherland on the Australian tour. Working alongside her every day for four months, Luciano was amazed by her ability to sing for up to eight hours at a stretch without any sign of tiring. He was used in the ordinary way to sleeping until midday, but on tour

rehearsals started at ten in the morning and Joan could run through the whole of *Traviata*, calmly embroidering cushions as she sang, and then performed in the evening with her voice still perfectly fresh. He realized that she must have some special means of producing the sound which reduced the strain on the vocal cords and gave her perfect control of her breathing. To learn her secret he would put his hands on her abdomen during off-stage rehearsals to feel her muscle action when she sang, and she taught him exercises to strengthen the key muscles supporting the rib cage and thus prolong the life of the voice. He worked hard at them until the technique became automatic, and he has never had problems with his breathing since.

The tour took them to Sydney, Melbourne, Adelaide and Brisbane, and they played to packed houses throughout. Luciano had never worked so hard in his life but he loved every minute of it. He was very fit, and whenever there was a free minute he went swimming in the ocean, played football or did handstands on the beach. I travelled with him for the first two months of the tour, leaving Lorenza and Cristina with my mother-in-law, Adele; it was the first time I had been away from them for so long. Cristina was only ten months old when we left – she had her first birthday just after I returned – and Lorenza was two and beginning to talk. Adele sent us a tape of her voice to keep us in touch with her progress and it made Luciano cry to listen to it, but what upset me even more was seeing no sign of recognition on Cristina's little face when the children were brought to meet me at the airport, and having to say 'It's Mamma' to remind her.

Since Luciano's first professional engagement in Lucca in 1961 I had been put in charge of the family's finances, and any money we could save had been set aside to buy a house of our own. In 1963 we had moved from the rented apartment

opposite my father's to a larger one nearby, which we shared with my sister Giovanna and her family, and after the Australian tour two years later we moved again, this time to our own villa in the southern outskirts of Modena, close to our present house. Luciano wrote out his first cheque as a down payment, and in the excitement of the moment absent-mindedly left for an engagement leaving it unsigned. We were hardly the bank's most valued customers but they were sympathetic and agreed to accept it.

For Italians, though it has lost a little of its legendary magic in recent years, La Scala in Milan has always had a special importance, and up to that time Luciano had had no opportunity to make his real début there. He had understudied Gianni Raimondi in *Traviata* and *Bohème*, but had not yet been offered a part in his own right that he felt confident of undertaking without fear of damaging his voice. One day he rang the bell outside the house to bring me to the window, and I looked down to see him standing in the garden with an excited grin on his face, waving in one hand a sheet of the distinctive pink paper on which only La

Scala contracts are printed and in the other a lemon squeezer which he had wanted for months but felt we could not afford. He had been signed up to play the Duke in *Rigoletto* and Rodolfo in *La Bohème* during the winter season of 1965–6. They liked him so much that he was invited back in the spring to take the role of Tebaldo in Bellini's *I Capuleti e i Montecchi*.

La Scala had an exchange arrangement with the Staatsoper in Vienna, where Herbert von Karajan was resident conductor, whereby young singers were 'borrowed' whenever the need arose, and although Luciano had been given few opportunities to sing at La Scala he had been sent by them several times to Vienna. It was Karajan who asked him to take part in a performance of the Verdi

TOP LEFT *Outside La Scala, Milan, 28 January 1966, where tickets for his performances of* La Bohème *were 'Tutto esaurito' – sold out.*
TOP RIGHT *As the Duke in* Rigoletto, *his first leading role at La Scala, December 1965.*

ABOVE LEFT *As Tebaldo in Bellini's* I Capuleti e i Montecchi *with Giacomo Aragall and Mario Petri, La Scala, April 1966.*
ABOVE RIGHT AND OPPOSITE *Publicity portraits taken in 1966.*

RIGHT ABOVE *At home with Lorenza (left), who was four, and Cristina, two, a few days after the birth of our third daughter, Giuliana, in January 1967.*

RIGHT BELOW *On holiday at Pesaro, August 1967: Luciano with Lorenza, Cristina and, in the pram, Giuliana. When we were young both Luciano and I were taken by our parents to the Adriatic resorts of the Marche region – Viserba, Rimini, Cattolica, Pesaro – and after we married we took our own children there; now we have a house at Pesaro which we use every summer.*

ABOVE *Luciano at home with me in October 1967, on a short break between trips to Montreal with La Scala's production of* I Capuleti e i Montecchi *and to San Francisco for* La Bohème.

RIGHT *Helping with the candles at Lorenza's fifth birthday party, 26 October 1967.*

Requiem at La Scala in January 1967 to mark both the centenary of Toscanini's birth and the tenth anniversary of his death. To appear there on such a prestigious occasion, and to work with the magnificent cast Karajan had lined up – Nicolai Ghiaurov, Fiorenza Cossotto and Leontyne Price – was a tremendous honour for anyone with as little experience as Luciano had at that time. Karajan loved to work with young people but his reputation was awe-inspiring; a rebuke from him would have been more mortifying than from almost any other conductor and Luciano took care to go extremely well prepared. Karajan was impressed, and they worked together many times after that, at the Staatsoper in Vienna, at La Scala in Milan and at the Salzburg Festival.

It was while Luciano was at La Scala for the Requiem that our third daughter, Giuliana, was born (with three daughters I have at least kept up the quota of females in his family). I had given up my job when I was pregnant with Cristina and begun to involve myself more closely in Luciano's career, handling his rapidly increasing flow of fan mail and accumulating an archive from the piles of publicity material and press cuttings that he brought back from foreign tours.

By now his career seemed to have a momentum of its own. Having sung *La Bohème* to great acclaim in San Francisco in November 1967, Luciano was asked to make his début with it at the Metropolitan Opera House in New York in November of the following year. He had made his mark at Covent Garden and La Scala; now he had to do the same at the Met. A big success at the Met is almost a prerequisite for any opera singer hoping to make an international name, and for the American public it is also a yardstick against which all other successes are measured. In addition to the pressure that this itself imposes, the knowledge that you must please the often acerbic

New York critics and that you will be singing to an audience of 4,200 people can make it a paralysing experience. Shortly before he was due in New York Luciano contracted a devastating dose of Hong Kong flu. With eyes streaming and a temperature of 102, he was miserably dejected, but he could not bear the thought of cancelling the engagement and managed to arrange a compromise

Luciano with a camera-shy Lorenza on her first day at the local scuola elementare, *1 October 1968.*

by postponing it for a week. He survived the first performance, and even had good reviews, but by the following evening he was worse and had to be replaced after the second act. He cancelled all his other New York commitments, took a plane home without even ringing me first to let me know he was coming – something he had never done before – and turned up on the doorstep with a look of such desolation on his face that I thought he must have been booed off the stage.

He had to wait five years to make up for the disappointment of his début at the Met, but when he returned with Joan Sutherland in 1972, in Covent Garden's production of *La Fille du Régiment*, he had the sort of history-making triumph that he had longed for. I was there on the first night with our three daughters, and it was a wonderful, unforgettable occasion. He and Joan were dazzling together and had spectacular fun doing it, Luciano riveting the audience to their seats with his nine high Cs in one aria. The papers next day were full of it. This was the beginning of a relationship with the New York public that has strengthened over the years into one of the most satisfying of his career, and his success at the Met that night helped to establish him in the eyes of the world as one of the greatest tenors of the century.

Joan Sutherland – known as La Stupenda – in the role of Marie and Luciano as Tonio in their triumphantly successful La Fille du Régiment, *conducted by Richard Bonynge, at the Metropolitan Opera House, New York, December 1972.*

'Whether he is talking with friends, a hotel porter or an audience of millions on a television talk show, Luciano is unaffected and genuine and people love him for it. He never sets out to impress, and his ability to cut through artificiality and make contact on a personal level is something to which everyone responds.'

4 A Natural Communicator

One of Luciano's most appealing natural assets as a performer is his ability to transmit his love of life and people to an audience; he is not afraid of emotions, and this comes across both in his singing and in his response to the public. He knows very well that it is his fans who have made him the success he has become, and takes every opportunity to repay them for taking him to their hearts so unreservedly. However tired he may be after a performance he always insists on greeting them, refusing to leave the theatre until he has done so, and will regularly spend two or three hours signing autographs and talking to the queues of people clamouring for him at the stage door. If he is dragged away to an official

reception he is always upset because to him the fans are more important; they may have come hundreds of miles to see him and waited for hours or even days to buy a ticket, and he wants to show them how much that means to him. Many of his admirers travel all over Europe or America, some even around the world to hear him sing and we see them wherever he appears.

One of his greatest fans until she died at the age of eighty-seven was a woman who lived at Senigallia in the Marche region, not far south of our summer

The Great Hall of the People in Tiananmen Square, the spectacular setting for a concert in Peking during a tour of China in 1986.

ABOVE *Luciano is especially delighted when young people respond to his music. After a concert in Barcelona on 6 September 1990, organized by Tibor Rudas (centre), he spent hours talking to a crowd of eager children.*
BELOW *Signing autographs in a Pesaro street.*

house at Pesaro. Throughout the last ten years of her life she devoted most of her energies to writing to Luciano and most of her small income as a pensioner to telephoning him (her son told me recently that he paid an enormous phone bill which was owing when she died). For years she also wrote regularly to RAI, the Italian broadcasting corporation, complaining because she did not hear Luciano Pavarotti on the radio every day, as she would have liked. Eventually she decided she must meet him, and in August 1975 she invited us both and our three daughters to a big lunch party which she organized in his honour at a hotel in Senigallia. As a special tribute, she arranged for a telegram to be delivered to him in the course of the meal expressing her joy at having Luciano at her lunch table. He was very touched by this gesture as he was not then the celebrated Pavarotti he has since become. After that she came every summer for dinner with us at Pesaro and once or twice to Modena, and since she died her son and daughter-in-law have paid us regular visits in order to maintain the friendship, which was important to us all.

The stream of press cuttings from around the world, which in the early days I handled myself, has swelled to a torrent in recent years, and since I now run an agency for young singers, Stage Door Opera Management, which occupies me full-time, the task of maintaining the archive has to be shared between other members of the family, four secretaries and a band of helpful volunteers. Between us we also handle all Luciano's correspondence with his fans. Hundreds of presents from admirers arrive for him

OPPOSITE *The Arena at Verona packed to capacity for* La Gioconda, *July 1980, in which Luciano played Enzo Grimaldo and Ghena Dimitrova the title role.*

in the course of the year, with an avalanche around Christmas and his birthday – portraits and sculptures of him, articles of clothing, hand-embroidered handkerchiefs – showing how much trouble people are prepared to take in order to demonstrate their devotion. We send out stacks of signed photographs daily in response to written requests and, at Luciano's insistence, answer every one of the dozens of fan letters which arrive by every post, many of them personally because they touch us so deeply. Not all come from opera fans; some of the most heart-rending have been written by sad and lonely people who have found comfort in his singing when they were in despair and life seemed not worth living. On Luciano's tour of Scandinavia in 1987 we arrived at our hotel at Göteborg in Sweden to find a telephone message from a young woman saying that a friend of hers, a girl of twenty-nine with a husband and two young children, was in hospital with incurable cancer, and that her dying wish was to speak to Luciano. He rang immediately and talked to her, and the next day, at her request, a bouquet of white flowers arrived at the hotel with a note of thanks. By the time he received them the girl had died.

Whether he is talking with friends, a hotel porter or an audience of millions on a television talk show, Luciano is unaffected and genuine and people love him for it. He never sets out to impress, and his ability to cut through artificiality and hype and make contact on a personal level is something to which everyone responds. His natural sincerity helps him to communicate his love of music, and also to overcome some of the barriers that have made opera the exclusive preserve of the privileged. Through his free concerts, recordings and televised performances he can reach an audience who might be daunted by the expense or the mere idea of an evening at the opera, but who love the mixture of arias and classic

ABOVE *In Tiananmen Square, Peking, 1986.*
BELOW *Luciano with our three, now adult, daughters, who came with us to China, in the gardens of the Summer Palace, Peking.*
OPPOSITE '*Making contact on a personal level*'.

songs that he offers them. His concert formula has introduced them not only to many of the greatest arias of the lyric tenor repertoire but also to beautiful music by neglected composers such as Tosti and Respighi, and to the warmth and vigour and intensity of a whole range of Neapolitan songs less familiar than 'Torna a Surriento' and 'O sole mio'. Luciano has always been drawn to the songs of Naples and is lucky to have this wonderful treasure-store of popular music at his disposal.

Of his many concerts of the last few years, some stand out as especially memorable because of the overwhelming response of the audience. Among them are Peking in 1986 and Buenos Aires in 1987. I travelled with him on both of these occasions, together with various members of the family and a few close friends, and of course a full orchestra and chorus.

It was an extraordinary experience to be greeted in a country as distant as China with quite so much open-hearted enthusiasm. At the airport when we arrived in Peking, and again when we were photographed in Tiananmen Square, we were surrounded by an endless sea of waving, cheering Chinese on bicycles, all eager to welcome Luciano to their country. He had been booked to give two performances of *La Bohème* and two recitals in Peking, and it was two days before the second recital that we were invited to a private lunch by the General Secretary of the Communist Party, Hu Yao Bang. Luciano was asked to name the largest theatre in which he had ever performed and replied that, aside from stadia and arenas, it was the Metropolitan Opera House in New York. He was told that the demand for tickets for his second recital was so phenomenal that, rather than holding it in a normal concert hall as had been planned, the Chinese Government would like to offer him instead the Great Hall of the People in Tiananmen Square. This vast building is used for

public assemblies and had never in history been opened for an event of this kind. Its capacity is over ten thousand, and the recital was sold out in a single day. Luciano was greeted on stage by Hu Yao Bang, and all the chief Party dignitaries were present in the audience. As usual, the programme consisted of arias from opera and popular Italian songs, most of them evidently as well known in China as they are in the West. The Neapolitans seem to have exported 'O sole mio', along with their pizzas, to every corner of the globe, and in China the first notes were greeted with as much delight as anywhere. Next to me was a ninety-year-old man, dressed in beige tunic and sandals, who had taken part in the Long March of 1934–5, which helped to bring the Chinese Communists to power under Mao Tse-tung. At the end of the recital, when the entire audience rose to applaud, he made a great effort to rise with them, and although I begged him to sit he took my arm, determined to stand and honour Luciano.

For all of us China was special; it was a new and exciting experience to go there and we found such boundless warmth

Luciano's delight in making music was reflected in the faces of the thousands of Chinese people who attended his two solo concerts in Peking.

and generosity in the people that we shall always want to return.

Perhaps the response in Argentina was a little less surprising because so many Italians had emigrated to South America during the first half of this century, but we were nonetheless unprepared for it. After several performances of *La Bohème* at Colon in August 1987, Luciano gave an arena concert at Luna Park, Buenos Aires, on 3 September. Ticket prices were kept as low as possible to avoid its becoming an event exclusively for Argentina's super-rich, and the audience of about fifteen thousand included a large percentage of immigrant Italians, many of whom had been sadly disappointed in their hopes of finding the streets of Buenos Aires paved with gold. The place was filled to overflowing, the stage and the entire arena decked out with red, white and green banners, the colours of our national flag, and the excitement in the air was electrifying. At the end of the concert the explosion of cheering and applause was so prolonged and emotional that all of us who witnessed it found our hearts gripped by the passion of the audience. As soon as Luciano left the stage the corridors to his dressing room filled with people eager to speak to him, among them a man originally from Modena who had left there many years before to find work in the building trade in South America. He had always lived in the hope of one day returning home, but had had to struggle to get by, and now that his son was married and settled in Argentina with children of his own it meant leaving them or living the rest of his life in exile from his beloved home town. He related his story in our local dialect, and tears of emotion streamed down his face as he repeatedly embraced Luciano and told him how much it had

meant to him to hear him sing. It was an experience that will stay with us for ever; we felt such close ties with the people, and they had shown such intensity of feeling, that within our group of family and friends we found our relationships strengthened because we had shared it.

Every performer needs to know that he has pleased the public, and for Luciano this is perhaps particularly true. After a performance of *L'Elisir d'Amore* at the Deutsche Oper in Berlin on 24 February 1988 a piano was brought onto the stage and he gave an impromptu recital because the audience simply re-fused to leave. They applauded for an hour and seven minutes and he was called back to the stage 165 times. This remark-able event has been recorded on the safety curtain of the theatre, and appears in the Guinness Book of Records for 1991 as the longest applause ever re-ceived by a solo performer.

The Three Tenors Concert, held on 7 July 1990 at the Baths of Caracalla in Rome to mark the end of the Italia '90 World Cup, was the inspired idea of José Carreras. He invited Placido Domingo and Luciano to take part – all three of them great football fans – and they

Placido Domingo, José Carreras and Luciano in rehearsal for the Three Tenors Concert which was held in Rome on 7 July 1990 to celebrate the Italia '90 World Cup.

responded with alacrity. There is great mutual respect between them and they regarded the occasion as a wonderful opportunity to perform together. They were all in top form on the night, and it became an extraordinary celebration of their talent as well as of the event itself. José had only recently recovered from leukaemia and resumed his singing

LEFT *The floodlit Baths of Caracalla in Rome made a magnificent backdrop for the orchestras of the Teatro dell' Opera di Roma and the Maggio Musicale Fiorentino at the Three Tenors Concert. The flautist Andrea Griminelli can be seen accompanying Luciano in the song 'Rondine al nido'.*
RIGHT *Luciano greets the conductor Zubin Mehta on stage.*
ABOVE *At the end of a spectacularly successful evening. As is the case with all Luciano's arena recitals, a percentage of the proceeds was donated to charity.*

career, and I found it very moving to sit surrounded by both his and Placido's families and to know that we were witnessing something brilliant and unforgettable, performed in a spirit of fun, affection and generosity. The concert was broadcast live around the world, and has been shown on American television alone at least four times, with international video, cassette and record sales exceeding seven million copies. An enormous sum has been offered by the Japanese for a repeat performance of the Three Tenors Concert at the Imperial Gardens in Tokyo, but Luciano has declined it because he believes the event would be diminished by repetition.

This particular concert served as a dramatic confirmation in the eyes of the public that Luciano is a man who takes joy in communicating, and it opened up possibilities of extending his love of music to an even wider audience. His open-air recital in London's Hyde Park on 30 July 1991 was free for all but the small percentage of people who elected to pay for seats near the stage, and it attracted a crowd of over 100,000. This was far fewer than predicted, but some were inevitably deterred by the fact that the night was the wettest in England for weeks. Londoners may be used to the rain but to stand for hours in a downpour shows a little more than British stoicism, and Luciano was astonished and moved by their unquenchable enthusiasm and by the welcome he received in Britain. The recital was funded largely by the sale of television and recording rights, and was broadcast live by satellite to thirty-three countries worldwide.

ABOVE *Despite the torrential summer rain, crowds gathered several hours before the open-air concert held in London's Hyde Park on 30 July 1991.*

On stage at Hyde Park. Having basked in the sun at Pesaro for a few weeks before the concert, Luciano was in good voice, and for him the rain was a bonus as it clears the air of dust and helps to relax the vocal cords.

'*His head thrown back
and a broad grin on
his face, he zooms round
the house and along the
terrace, hooting loudly
as he careers off down
the drive to the beach.*'

5 Zest for Life

I firmly believe that in everyone who achieves real distinction as a performer there are exceptional human qualities, and it is this that lifts them above the ranks of those who have only talent. To be a professional singer, not necessarily even a great singer, you must have innate musicality, intelligence, perseverance and a belief in yourself, you must be a little daring and, just as importantly, you must have practically inexhaustible stamina in order to withstand the pressures of this most demanding career — and that is in addition of course to the voice. Luciano has all these qualities or he would never have achieved the ranks of *primo tenore*, but he has something more: the personality is as big as the man and there is no doubt that it has contributed much to his success.

Although he is full of contradictions, he is in many respects, in the eyes of foreigners at least, a typical Italian, with all the good and bad that that implies: he is warm-hearted, sociable, spontaneous, exuberant and disastrously over-indulged by the many women in his family. Luciano is drawn to women young and old, and in general prefers their company and conversation to that of men. After all we make ourselves very useful: at home there is always a house full of helpers to wait on him, to fetch him a drink, to find his pen, to pick up his glasses, to hand him the telephone, to fill in his diary or search for a scarf. Surrounded by adoring women as a child, he almost inevitably grew up with a conviction that domestic tasks are the province of females and with an intractable reluc-

On holiday at our house at Pesaro, August 1991. The scooter was Luciano's latest acquisition, and it delighted him.

tance to share them. I was brought up by a father who had been left a widower in his late thirties with three young children to care for, and who had learned as a result to be a great deal more domesticated than most Italian men of his generation; since I had no brothers I had never been fully aware of the privileges and importance traditionally accorded to boys in my country, and was therefore quite unprepared for life with Luciano. I did my best at the beginning to persuade him to cooperate just a little on the domestic front, but he had never been asked to do anything that he did not want to do, and of course a career as an opera singer was calculated only to make things worse as the years went by. I sometimes say '*È tutto colpa di tua nonna*' – it is all the fault of your grandmother – but really it was the consequences of over-indulgence of the male of the species by generations of women before her that I inherited in Luciano.

Enjoying a gift from a visitor – a photographic profile of Picasso – with two of his family of females, our daughter Cristina and I, in attendance.

The love that surrounded him as a child made him feel that life was good and he had no need to defend himself against it. It also gave him a sense of his own worth. He was always number one, and that made him determined to win, to accept nothing but first place. We often play cards in the evening with family and friends – usually a simple game known as *briscola* – with the stakes set at no more than a few lire (perhaps the equivalent of ten pence). Luciano simply has to win, even if he has to cheat to do so, and is very put out if he doesn't, which makes us try all the harder to beat him.

I think some people who know only his public face are surprised to learn that by nature he is contemplative because this aspect of his character appears to be at odds with his exuberance; perhaps it is in fact a means of feeding it. Like his father, he is capable of spending hours without moving from a chair, but his brain is always active, generating new ideas which demand feverish activity on the part of other people. Wherever he is, he is the pivot around which all life revolves.

It is not only women but men too who respond to his charm and charisma,

Luciano plays to win and
employs every tactical resource he
can muster in order to outwit his
opponents at briscola.

which can be hard to resist. He is in fact instinctively democratic, but I suspect that if he ever devised a political manifesto it would describe a utopian world benevolently run by Luciano Pavarotti. He does genuinely need his regiment of helpers because he is horribly untidy and disorganized: papers and possessions are strewn over every available surface, and he is perfectly capable of booking two appointments for the same time and forgetting both of them. He does, on the other hand, have an almost infallible memory for the written word, an invaluable asset for an opera singer. He can still quote extracts from the odes of Ovid and Horace that he learnt at school, and although he is not a great reader he remembers in detail books that he read

Personal friendships mean a great deal to Luciano. With Franco Casarini, whom he has known since 1961, he shares his passion for both opera and football; they frequently travel together on tour, and Franco has many times helped Luciano in the research required for new recording work.

many years ago. His ear for music and rhythm has helped to imprint them on his brain, and his work by its very nature keeps his memory active. Travelling as much as he does, he meets new people all over the world, but he hardly ever fails to remember a place or a face or a name. We went to Mexico not long ago and met the manager of a bank whom Luciano recalled instantly as someone he had been at school with in Modena thirty years before, while I can fail, to my shame, to place even people I know quite well if I see them out of context. Everyone is flattered to be recognized, particularly by those they admire, and his fans appreciate it immensely when he remembers them.

Luciano has a phenomenal capacity for enjoying himself, and a determination

not to put off until tomorrow anything he can enjoy today. *Carpe diem* – seize the day – is his philosophy. In the 1940s, when he was young, food was scarce, especially butter (*emiliano* butter, among the best in Italy, is used for pasta-making, so fulfilled a vital need), but Luciano would spread it thickly on slices of bread, replying to Nonna Giulia's warnings that there might be no more tomorrow, 'But we're here today; no one knows if we'll be here tomorrow.' We have an expression in Italian, '*Meglio un uovo oggi che una gallina domani*' – better an egg today than a hen tomorrow – which sums up his belief in living for the moment. When we were first married and could afford very little, he was content to enjoy to the full the life that we had without ever

Established in his usual seat on the terrace at Pesaro, August 1991, equipped with books, glasses, diary, a drink and a complete boxed set of pipes.

wanting what was then out of reach, and he has never altered in this respect. Circumstances, however, have changed dramatically and few things are now out of reach, yet this has done nothing to moderate his desire to enjoy all that life has to offer before the day is out.

His need to gratify other people's desires is just as immediate: if someone dear to him says, 'I would like ...', he goes at once to buy it for them. Recently it was pipes. He likes to smoke a pipe sometimes after a meal, and our youngest daughter, Giuliana, and my assistant, Francesca Barbieri, both said they would like to try it. We were at our summer house at Pesaro on the Adriatic coast, the pipes were in Modena, so a new boxed set had to be bought that very day.

He develops equally urgent and insatiable passions for certain items of clothing. If he finds some shoes that he likes he is convinced he will live in them for the rest of his life and buys several identical pairs. And his love of scarves is well known. A few years ago they had to be long and narrow, made of fine wool; now they are vast squares, designed by Hermès, as flamboyant as the banners in a medieval pageant, and he drapes them around him – sometimes several at a time – with a confident disregard of the fashion and an uninhibited instinct for self-expression. After a press conference in Florence last year he left a scarf on a chair, and all the newspapers carried the news that Pavarotti had lost a scarf, his favourite scarf, with the result that he was deluged with replacements in every conceivable size and colour.

He has enormous collections of everything and will never get rid of a single item in case one day he might need it. This makes no allowance, of course, for the fact that houses do not have elastic walls and that one cannot be forever buying wardrobes. When he comes home from a tour with twice as many suitcases as he took away with him – in order to accommodate all the presents he has bought for himself and other people, as well as all those he has been given – space has to be found not only for the presents but also for the suitcases. Fortunately we have an extended family and someone always needs a suitcase, but from time to time I threaten to set up a stall in the market or apply for a licence to run a travelling shop in order to dispose of the overflow. If he sees a new scooter in a catalogue, as he did the other day at Pesaro, there is no time to go to the store and try it out; Luciano has to have it now, and when it is delivered he enjoys it with the unselfconscious abandon of a

OVERLEAF *Luciano is happy to give rides on his scooter to anyone who shares his sense of fun, on this occasion José Carreras, who visited us at Pesaro, August 1991.*

*Spontaneous,
optimistic and
extrovert by
nature, he has
an openness of
outlook and
a zest for life
that allows
him to extract
the best from
every encounter.*

Luciano with his red mercedes – which is not so much a status symbol as a reflection of his own exuberance – beside the harbour at Pesaro, August 1991.

five-year-old, taking anyone who is brave or crazy enough to go with him – including Anna, who cooks for us, and his friend José Carreras – for rides on the back. Wearing a Hawaiian shirt and a sunhat, his head thrown back and a broad grin on his face, he zooms round the house and along the terrace, hooting loudly as he careers off down the drive to the beach. Fortunately he has never developed a mania for cars, or worse, partly because his buying habits have nothing to do with showing off what he

can afford, simply a desire to live life to the full. They are also an expression of his ability to throw himself without reserve into any new passion, just as he did when he began to study singing.

He adopts a positive attitude to almost everything and has little time for anyone who fails to make the most of life. It exasperates him to hear young people complain about what is wrong with the world instead of appreciating what is right with it, and he is convinced that if they had to fight a little harder for a comfortable existence they would realize how much they have to be thankful for. It was in part the Second World War that formed Luciano's philosophy because it taught him that life is not something to

be taken for granted. It also gave him a distrust of the powers of political persuasion: as a child he knew a man who killed his brother because they were on opposing sides, one a partisan, the other a Fascist, and he still believes that no political cause should take precedence over love and loyalty to the family. Like all of us in Italy, he has seen governments come and go and life carry on as it has always done, and while he is deeply disturbed by social injustice he has little faith in party politics to ensure a fairer distribution of the world's resources.

His genuine love of his fellow man is combined with a generosity of spirit that enables him to see the good in everyone. He is almost invariably generous in his appraisal of other singers and never attends a performance in order to listen to their weaknesses, only their strengths. He shows a touching concern for other people's welfare, going to great lengths, for example, to find the right doctor or seek out appropriate treatment for someone he knows who is ill. (He is also capable, however, of ringing up a friend in the middle of the night because he is in a different time zone and feels like a chat.)

A very traditional Italian in many respects, Luciano's first concern is always for the family, partly because he knows from his own experience the value of the security and warmth it can provide. That security gave him great confidence. He is a man of few misgivings, very much at ease with himself, very natural, very honest, always convinced that good will triumph, and if things go wrong he accepts the outcome philosophically. His only real anxieties are professional ones. Whatever heights he has already achieved as a lyric tenor, he is constantly striving to attain his own individual ideals.

Luciano astride a toy horse made by an American friend and intended as a present for one of our youngest relations.

*'He loves to have
people around, and
rather than trying
to escape them when we go to Pesaro in the summer
he makes up for his weeks away from friends
and family by inviting everyone to stay.'*

6 A Family Man

Luciano's family ties have always been strong, and when we moved to our present house in Modena in 1978 it was his dream to gather all his close family together, if not under one roof then at least within shouting distance. We have almost achieved it. It is a spacious house, once the centre of a large estate, and was built around 1800 in the traditional style of the region – four-square, with a small central tower, originally a dovecote, and an outbuilding alongside it which provided stabling for the farm. The house is approached by a straight drive through a plantation of poplars, and around it stretches the flat arable land of the Modena plain. The whole place was run down when we bought it, and the first

thing we did was restore the main house for ourselves, making a separate apartment upstairs for my sister Giovanna and her family. We then turned the outbuilding into apartments for Luciano's parents, his sister Gabriella and her son Luca, and a number of other relations.

We are a close-knit family, even by Italian standards, and Luciano loves to know that he has provided the means of uniting us still further. The house at Modena exerts a gravitational pull, and he returns to it as often as he can, usually managing to snatch a few days' break

Lunch on the terrace, the focus of our days at Pesaro, with Luciano regularly presiding over large gatherings of family and friends.

every four or five weeks between tours, and wherever he is he telephones once if not several times a day for an exchange of news.

Our three daughters live with us at home, and this makes it easier to avoid the sort of gaps in understanding that inevitably occur when relationships are disrupted by periods apart. Lorenza, the eldest, has her own dress shop in Modena and the two younger ones are at Bologna University, Cristina studying literature and the performing arts and Giuliana physical education. It has not always been easy for them to be the daughters of Luciano Pavarotti, and when they were little they wished he was rather more like other children's fathers. To compensate

ABOVE *Luciano at home in Modena. The house stands on the southern outskirts of the town, only two kilometres from his birthplace.*
OPPOSITE *The plantation of Lombardy poplars flanking the approach to the house. We planted the trees soon after we moved here in 1978, and now their tall trunks filter the summer sunlight and give us an area of cool shade close to the house.*

for his absences, he was indulgent in his affection and never disciplined them: 'I spend so little time at home, it would seem as if I only come back to punish them', he used to say. He even got upset with me if I attemped to correct them – if for instance I asked them to tidy their rooms (and they are all as untidy as their father) – yet it annoyed him to see them do things differently from the way he would have wished. I suppose we are all of us a little inconsistent.

Family decisions of any real importance we have always taken jointly, unless we cannot agree, in which case Luciano generally has the final word, but matters concerning the children, such as what subjects they should study at

A local painter frescoed the ceilings of the living room – in which we had the curved staircase installed – the entrance hall and the dining room. In the study is a grand piano, which is occasionally played by Cristina, and is used by both Luciano and his father in their routine vocal exercises.

ABOVE *The entrance to our Modena house, with a family dog – one of several – genially failing to endorse the notice on the gate.*
RIGHT *The traditional three-storey villa dates from 1800; painted in ochre and white, with symmetrical windows and porticoes and a central turret, it is typical of its time and place. Together with a large outbuilding, it now houses twenty members of the Pavarotti family.*

ABOVE *The Villa Giulia, our house at Pesaro named after Luciano's grandmother, was originally a farmhouse, which we converted when we acquired the property in 1974.*

Luciano at the centre of our extended family at Pesaro, August 1991.

From left to right: (back row) my brother-in-law Gaetano Ballerini, our cook Anna Antonelli and her son Ferdinando, Donatella Bettinelli (the daughter of my eldest sister Loredana) and my sister Giovanna Ballerini; (middle row) Alberto Garcia Demestres (a friend of the family), Cristina, Luciano and I, Giuliana, Lorenza and my assistant Francesca Barbieri; (front row) Giorgio Antonelli (grandson of Anna and Angiolino), Lia Merli (granddaughter of Loredana), Gaia Bettinelli (daughter of Donatella) and Lia's brother, Alessandro Merli.

For Luciano holidays are precious above all because they allow him a rare opportunity to spend time with our three daughters.

ABOVE *Our eldest daughter, Lorenza, runs her own shop in Modena.*
ABOVE RIGHT *Cristina is studying literature and the performing arts at Bologna University.*
FAR RIGHT *Giuliana, the youngest – with her cousin Lia – is also at Bologna University studying physical education.*

school, have usually been settled by them; even when they were very young they had such clear ideas of their own that we often let them decide for themselves if the consequences of making mistakes were not serious.

The girls are three distinct and very different individuals (though they seem sometimes to be regarded by the press as interchangeable), but their upbringing, which has been so different from our own, has given them a shared outlook on certain issues. While we grew up in the war, and its aftermath affected all our expectations and priorities, they were born into a society whose preoccupations were more complex, and into a family whose way of life could hardly be described as average. The standard of living has changed at a bewildering speed in northern Italy over the past thirty

years, and in our family more than most. Naturally they appreciate the benefits that Luciano's success has brought to all of us – the fact that they have had the chance to see the world and have never wanted for anything material – but sometimes they might have preferred to stay at home with their friends instead of travelling, and to have led a saner life than the one they have been offered. Indeed they crave anonymity, and find exposure to the intrusive curiosity of strangers extremely irksome. They have an aversion to the idea of profiting from their position as Pavarotti's daughters, and in order to avoid being offered special treatment will often book a table in a restaurant in the name of one of their companions, or use my maiden name, as Cristina did last summer when she took part in a theatrical production in Spain.

Luciano, on the terrace that surrounds the Villa Giulia, against a background of the Baia Flaminia.

They have had to find their own ways of coping with the pressures of Pavarotti life, and in my opinion they have done so remarkably well. I derive a great deal of pleasure from the fact that they are as balanced, intelligent and natural as they are.

There are inevitably times when the pressures of Luciano's life intrude too much on their relationship with him, when every conversation is interrupted by visitors arriving and departing, by the telephone ringing, and by the constant activity that surrounds him wherever he is, but they have gradually adjusted to the fact that he is always in the public eye. They have a great respect for his work, never praising him for the sake of it, but

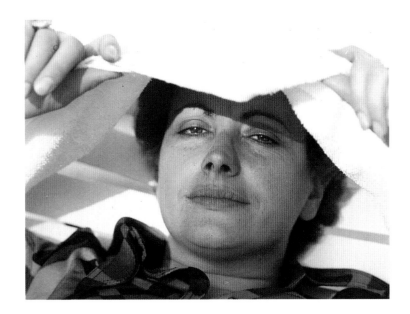

I long for a holiday isolated from every means of communication with the outside world, and any peaceful interludes in our day are gladly welcomed.

sometimes offering constructive comments on artistic interpretation in the light of what they have heard or seen him do on previous occasions. When he makes a new recording we all listen to it with a critical ear at various stages of production, and although his voice forms the musical background to our lives it has lost none of its power to move us. It is somehow more important to criticize something beautiful because you want it to be perfect than something bad which leaves a lot to be desired, and where their father's work is concerned the girls are perfectionists. He will often consider their suggestions afterwards, and adopt them if he believes them to be right, though at the time he usually pretends to have dismissed them.

When Luciano returns from a trip there are always a hundred things to fit into the few days before he leaves again, and even on holiday the pace hardly seems to slacken. He loves to have people around, and rather than trying to escape them when we go to Pesaro in the summer he makes up for his weeks away from friends and family by inviting everyone to stay. We bought the house there (known as Villa Giulia after Luciano's grandmother) in 1974, and set about converting it from a modest tenant farmer's house into a place where we could retreat with the family from Modena's suffocating midsummer heat. It stands on a hillside above the Baia Flaminia at one end of Pesaro, and looks out over the Adriatic Sea. When we acquired it it was inhabited by Anna and Angiolino Antonelli and their family, who worked for the local landowners to whom the house belonged. We made an apartment for them at one end of the building, and Angiolino and his son still work the land; Anna, undaunted as a result of years spent cooking dinners in a monastery, now cooks for us, helped by her daughter-in-law and two grandsons. They continue to live there all the year round as they have always done and we descend upon them for four to six weeks in the summer.

Since this is the only period of the year when, theoretically at least, Luciano is free and in the same place for more than a week at a time, visitors come in a ceaseless stream to work with him: journalists and photographers gather to do stories on him; young singers come to study with him; his *répétiteur* from the Met in New York, dear Gildo di Nunzio, stays for three weeks every year to rehearse him in the roles he will be singing there in the autumn; Herbert Breslin, his manager, comes to plan schedules for his forthcoming tours; or a party of German fans turns up to see where the great man spends his holidays, and sometimes they come armed with boxes of praline or gingerbread which have to be hastily eaten by everyone else before Luciano spots them. All this goes on against a background of family holiday life, with half-a-dozen nieces and nephews playing table tennis or wild games in the swimming pool, and is interspersed with extended lunches and dinners for anything up to twenty-five people at long tables on the terrace. After lunch Luciano retires to snooze in a

hammock slung between the trees, and, once recovered, resumes his usual vantage point overlooking the beach below the house, keeping his finger on the button to operate the automatic gates at the bottom of the drive. Beside him is the telephone and it is impossible to intervene when it rings and say that he is out because he always gets there first, and being hospitable by nature frequently invites the caller to the house.

One evening last July I was asked by a journalist how I would describe an average day in our lives at Pesaro, and although it had started a little earlier than usual – coffee at half-past eight with three technicians from Decca – that day seemed as representative as any and I briefly took her through it. Luciano had spent the first two hours of the morning, interrupted repeatedly by the ever-insistent telephone, working with the Decca crew on his recording of *Otello*. He

ABOVE *Luciano learns quickly but admits to having a short attention span, and his* répétiteur *from the Met seizes opportunities to work with him.*
ABOVE RIGHT *Studying the score of Mozart's* Idomeneo *in preparation for a production in New York.*

then had a meeting with the family accountant, made a deal with a local fisherman who turned up at the house with a quantity of shellfish, spent half an hour with a baritone from Washington who had come to study with him, and was snatched, as soon as a second's lull

occurred, by the patiently waiting Gildo for a few minutes' keyboard work in preparation for an engagement at the Met. This, punctuated at frequent intervals by a stream of new arrivals – his parents, my sister Giovanna, his sister Gabriella and her son Luca, and two

friends who dropped in unexpectedly — took us up to lunch time, when twenty-two of us sat down to *tagliatelle al ragù*, followed by *arrosto misto* (platters of roast chicken, veal and pork cutlets), green salad, fruit, a dish of cornetti pastries and finally coffee, all prepared and served by the redoubtable Anna. After another session with the Decca crew and a trim to the hair and beard by a visiting barber from Modena, Luciano left for a meeting in San Marino, from which he was not due back until late that night.

As we watched the car turn the bend at the bottom of the drive, peace descended briefly on the house, and it was then that the journalist arrived. We had been talking for half an hour on the terrace when out of a pale blue evening sky iron-dark clouds and a lurid light spread rapidly towards us and the fierce wind

FAR LEFT *An evening stroll along the beach with his great-nieces, Lia, aged five, and Gaia, three, August 1991.*

ABOVE *Luciano with his eleven-year-old great-nephew, Alessandro.*

LEFT AND BELOW *A trip around the bay in a motor boat which we keep moored in the harbour at Pesaro, with (left to right) Lorenza, Giuliana and Cristina. Luciano enjoys taking our family and friends water-skiing.*

ABOVE *The family table at a party to celebrate Cristina's twenty-seventh birthday, Pesaro, August 1991; (left to right) Francesca Barbieri, myself, Luciano, Lorenza, Giuliana with Alessandro on her lap, and Cristina.*
RIGHT *A game of cards with Giuliana by the pool.*

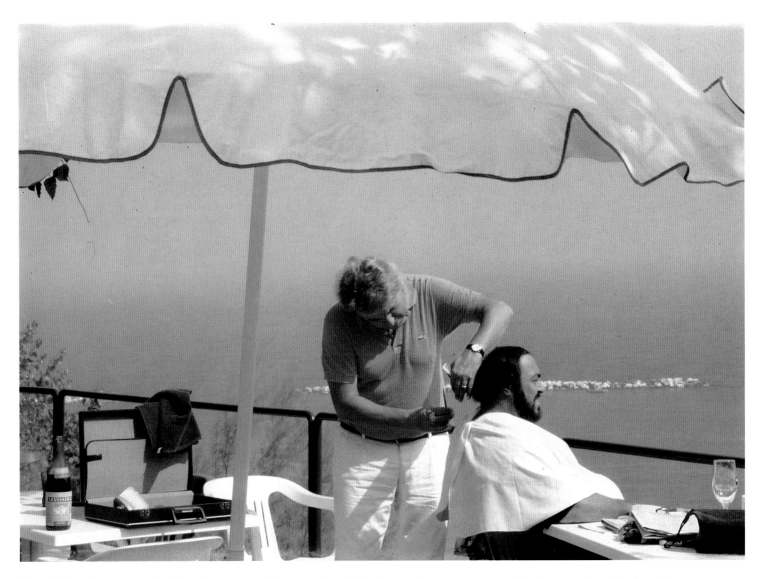

from Trieste known as the Bora began to whip up huge, white-crested waves in the bay. It hit us at hurricane force, sending everyone tearing in all directions after discarded shirts, coffee cups, towels and papers, piling up chairs and rescuing books and a forgotten child. No sooner had we all retreated inside than Angiolino could be heard yelling that the house was on fire. Lightning had struck the electric cables running down the side of the building, and acrid black smoke was pouring out of the top and bottom of the casing. Suddenly we were all outside again, shouting at the tops of our voices in order to be heard above the wind, while Anna, who speaks an Umbrian dialect that only Luciano fully understands, ran round the house issuing incomprehensible instructions to everyone she passed. Three fire engines, bells clanging, came roaring up the hill and spilt a tangle of hoses all over the terrace. A few minutes later, though we had no electricity and the house was awash with water and foam, relative calm had been restored, and Anna, having decided that the main excitement of the day was over, returned to preparations for the evening meal; amidst the debris of the hurricane and fire she was to be seen single-mindedly peeling potatoes in the last remaining daylight on the terrace. Shortly after that the journalist left, looking distinctly shell-shocked and saying she had learned enough about our average day to feel that hurricanes and electric storms were only to be expected.

Luciano remains at his favourite vantage point – seated on the terrace overlooking the beach – to receive the attentions of a modenese *barber.*

*Life at Pesaro
is a dizzying
existence for all
concerned;
though Luciano
happily thrives
on it, a
recuperative
snooze in the
hammock is an
essential feature
of the afternoon
routine.*

*'Luciano loves to eat
not just abundantly
but well, and this
necessitates consuming
generous samples of every dish before
it leaves the kitchen to ensure that it is
perfectly cooked and seasoned.'*

7   A Capacity for Pleasure

Luciano's enthusiasms have shown little sign of diminishing over the years; he finds outlets for the tensions of his working life in a range of outside interests, and likes to engage everyone around him in pursuing them to the full.

When we first met, sport was his chief passion aside from music, and although it has been largely a passive pleasure for some years now, it is one that still absorbs him deeply. As a child he played football in almost every free minute, and by his late teens he had developed the build and strength of an athlete and a fairly exceptional talent; in those days he played left wing or centre forward for Modena's 'Lepanto' team. An ardent supporter of Juventus of Turin all his life, he still goes occasionally to live matches, watches national and international football avidly on televisions all over the world, and wherever he is he telephones one of his oldest friends, Franco Casarini, in Italy every Sunday to hear the latest team results.

Luciano is a fan of anyone who excels at sport, and was thrilled when he was introduced to one of his childhood heroes, the great Argentinian Formula One motor-racing champion, Juan Manuel Fangio, on his trip to Buenos Aires in 1987. As a boy he had also admired Fausto Coppi and Gino Bartali, who made cycle racing popular in Italy in the 1940s and '50s, and when Bartali came to his dressing room after a concert at the Palasport Stadium in Florence in 1987, both Luciano and the conductor,

Painting has added a new dimension to Luciano's life in recent years and occupies him increasingly, both at home and on tour.

BELOW *Luciano used to say that if a horse was prepared to carry him he was happy to ride, and when he began building up his stable in the early 1980s he found a source of peace and relaxation in days spent in the country on one of his favourite hunters.*
RIGHT *Finding time to visit horses when away on tour: Tulsa, Oklahoma, 1981.*
FAR RIGHT *Though he no longer rides, he has an unusual rapport with horses and loves to spend time at our stables in Modena.*

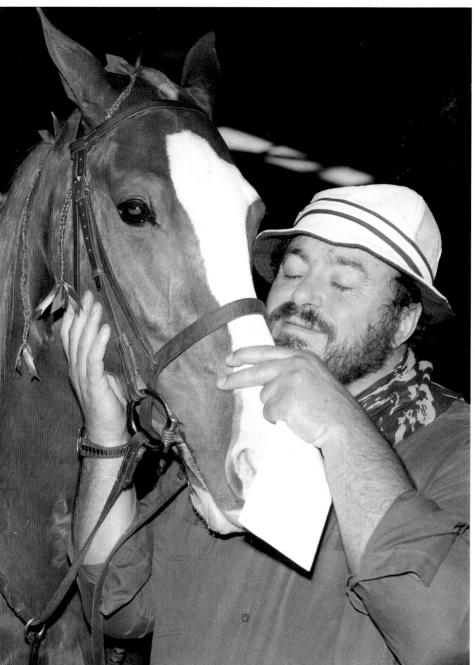

Leone Magiera, were wildly excited to meet him.

In recent years he has been free to indulge an early and abiding love of horses. When he was a boy he would beg to be allowed to go and stay with an uncle who had a pony and trap, and who bought and sold horses at markets in the local towns, but it was a trip to Dublin for a recital at the Gaiety Theatre in December 1979 that sparked off a more active interest. He was taken to the Iris

Kellett Riding School in Kildare, and eagerly rang me to say that I must persuade our three daughters to go over there and take lessons. In 1981 they duly went, flying for the first time on their own, and stayed at Miss Kellett's, getting up at seven in the morning to muck out the stables and ride. Giuliana still rides occasionally but none of us can be said to share Luciano's feeling for horses, which is dependent not so much on riding itself as on the pleasure to be derived from

contact with them and from watching them perform.

It was on his trip to Ireland in 1979 that he bought his first horses. Herbie, a four-year-old gelding and an excellent jumper, was acquired for Giuliana, and though eventually he settled down he was alarmingly frisky at first, and it frightened me to death to see him race off at a gallop with my youngest daughter on his back. Shaughran, at eighteen hands, was a massive and powerful hunter, quite

oblivious of Luciano's weight in the saddle. Bought from an English doctor who wanted to find him a good home, he was fourteen when he came to Modena and stayed with us until he died in 1987 at the great age of thirty-one. Gentle and well bred, he was used to town life and stopped of his own acccord at traffic lights and street junctions. In time three or four more horses were acquired. Originally they were kept in outbuildings close to the house, but they attracted

so many flies that when their numbers increased still further I insisted a range of riding stables should be built a little further away. Now Luciano has sixteen horses of his own, and a few belonging to other people are stabled with us, and although I take care of the administration of the stables I rather prefer not to think of the labour and expense involved in maintaining them.

Luciano's most recent, and most ambitious, equestrian venture is the Pavar-

otti International Horse Trials, held for the first time in mid-September 1991. Planned as an annual event and contracted initially for five years, we hope its early success will allow it to be repeated indefinitely. Funded entirely by commercial sponsorship, it was a massively complex undertaking, requiring a special ground to be laid out near our stables in Modena, stands to be built to seat four thousand people, restaurants and car parks to be provided and a number of

ABOVE *Luciano, Giuliana and I on the opening day of the Pavarotti International Horse Trials, held for the first time in September 1991.*

RIGHT *Posters in Modena advertising the event.*

LEFT *Luciano, to the left in the crowd, presenting awards.*

BELOW *Puffing a cigar as he watches the showjumping. Luciano enjoys an occasional pipe or cigar and firmly maintains that it does not harm his voice.*

LEFT *The Princess Royal, President of the International Equestrian Federation, was the guest of honour at a dinner held at the Military Academy in Modena on the penultimate day of the Trials, 14 September 1991.*

Though he eats very little on the day of a performance, in the evening Luciano makes up for his abstinence with a large, relaxing meal in the company of friends.

additional attractions besides, including music from the Salzburg Festival Orchestra and a Mexican choir. Of the Trials themselves, which took place over [a] four-day period, David Broome, who [h]eaded the British showjumping team [w]hich had won the World League [T]rophy in the Nations Cup of 1991), said, [']...ever have I seen a show like this; in [...]t in our world there's never been one.' [...]rounded by professional riders and [...]ers, and by horse-lovers from all [...] the world, Luciano was in an [...]ent that he loves, and it gave him [...]nous satisfaction to be able to at-[...]uch a gathering to Modena.

[Wh]en the stables were built in 1987 a [...]use was provided for the local [...]raternity, with a public restaurant [...] which is run by independent [...]ment. Luciano frequently holds [...]s there over lunch – a convenient

arrangement but one which encourages him to mix rather too much pleasure with his business. There is no denying that food is Luciano's Achilles' heel. A great deal has already been written and said about it, but it is not a subject one can easily avoid when discussing the principal pleasures of his life. It is a passion that he shares with his father, whose waking thoughts are dominated by two topics – music and food. When Fernando comes into our house in the morning for a coffee he frequently runs through a list of all that he plans to cook and eat in the course of the day. I have sometimes attempted to explain my husband's appetite by saying that it derives from the scarcity of food during the war, or that he eats as a means of relaxing from a stressful working life, but in truth this is no more than half the story: others lived through the same period without the

An equestrian clubhouse was built near our Modena stables in 1987, with an adjoining restaurant run as an independent venture by private management. Luciano takes full advantage of the facilities.

His interest in food has stimulated a talent for cooking, and he enjoys experimenting with new dishes.

OPPOSITE *Pasta is an indispensible element in Luciano's life.*
BELOW LEFT *Zubin Mehta consuming a plate of spaghetti cooked by Luciano, Israel, 1978.*
BELOW RIGHT *Cooking lunch in New York with* modenese *soprano Mirella Freni.*
BOTTOM LEFT *Both Luciano and his father are convinced of the need for an ample girth in order to sustain the power of the voice.*
BOTTOM RIGHT *Helping Kurt Adler (for many years director of the San Francisco Opera House) to another mouthful at a reception in Miami, Florida, April 1978.*

same result, and he loved food long before he became a singer. Maybe it is simply a reflection of his appetite for life; he is not a moderate man.

Luciano loves to eat not just abundantly but well, and this necessitates consuming generous samples of every dish before it leaves the kitchen to ensure that it is perfectly cooked and seasoned – a disaster for the waistline. He also enjoys shopping for food and is good at it, and although he tends to buy the most expensive items in the belief that they must be better, which is not of course always the case, he compensates for a bit of extravagance with his talent for making appetizing concoctions out of left-overs. He likes to cook, which can be helpful, but afterwards I invariably wish he hadn't. People say that when men cook they use every pan they can find and wash none of them up, but somehow in this as in all things my husband exceeds the normal limits. If he prepares a meal there is food on the walls as well as in the dishes, and clearing up the mess is not his speciality.

Spending weeks away from home can be solitary, particularly as Luciano cannot afford to run the risk of catching cold, and if the weather is bad he is often confined to his rooms for days at a time. Generally he rents an apartment rather than staying in a hotel because he likes to have plenty of space, and although he needs uninterrupted periods of study he also needs to relax with friends; preparing a meal provides a pleasant way of doing so. As Luciano's engagements at the Metropolitan Opera House require him to be in New York for several months of the year, we have an apart-

ment there which is stocked with enough food to withstand a long siege. New York is almost like home for us; it is full of friends. On the whole Luciano has an easy rapport with Americans, who tend to be a little like him – extrovert, positive, open to new ideas, convinced that everything is possible and must be made to happen fast. Europeans, by contrast, rooted in centuries of culture, are in less of a hurry, and are generally more complex in their responses, and Luciano likes the brash dynamism of American life.

One might imagine that trying out new restaurants abroad would be a great bonus of foreign tours, but Luciano rarely does so; it is inevitably difficult to escape the intrusions of the press, and

Giuliana and Cristina in New York with their father, April 1991, for his performances of Otello *at the Metropolitan Opera House.*

hordes of predatory photographers snapping round the table do diminish the pleasures of an evening out. Though he loves to sample the cuisine of other countries, he cannot survive for long without his traditional *modenese* dishes.

So great in fact is his need for regular supplies of Italian food that when we went to China in 1986 he made it a condition of the tour that the basic ingredients necessary to the making of certain authentic dishes should be transported with us to Peking. I tried to reason with him that we were unlikely to go hungry, and that if we did it would be good for him because it would be a way of losing weight. It was not that he doesn't like Chinese food – he does – it was simply that the thought of no Italian food at all, for a whole fortnight, brought on a feeling of panic. The orchestra and chorus of the Teatro Margherita in Genoa was to accompany us on the tour, and next door to the theatre is a very famous restaurant, Zefferino's. To my horror, Luciano organized with them the transportation of fresh vegetables and fruit, pasta, Sardinian pecorino and mature parmesan, Ligurian olive oil and ten kilos of *pesto alla genovese* (Genoa's traditional basil sauce) together with refrigerators, pots and pans, and all the other essential paraphernalia. The arrangements were personally supervised by Signor Zefferino, who came with us to Peking, accompanied by a chef to prepare some of the restaurant's specialities. When we arrived at our hotel it was logical, since my husband and I had more space than other members of our party, to store the food in our suite, and for several nights I clambered over crates of tortellini and slept surrounded by aubergines and jars of olives, the air heavy with the smell of rotting melons.

Luciano is always most concerned that his neighbour at table should have enough to eat (which does not, however, prevent him from sneaking food off my plate), and although many people are touched by his anxiety for their welfare, some do prefer – and even need – to eat lightly. A cousin of mine who had a delicate stomach and was used to eating and drinking very little, suffered severe pains as a result of over-indulging at dinner with us one evening and was taken quite ill. Luciano has ceased to be so pressing since dieting has become part of his life, but he still imagines that food matters as much to others as it does to him. On one occasion recently I was in Modena for a few days before joining

For Luciano much of
the appeal of painting
lies in the fact that it is
creative rather than
interpretative, and that
it offers him a means of
self-expression and
fulfilment which is
independent of other
people.

e early stages of a diet, when he finds it
...lt to sleep at night, it fills the
hours and provides an invaluable
...om eating. It is the perfect
...meone who spends days
...n, needs to find relax-
...ures of work and
...n ounce to his

...o, where
...of the
...uc-

L.
to pa...
without

this to use on stage a box of oil paints sent
to him by an admirer to mark his début in
the role. He found he had fun with them,
and gradually began to take painting a
little more seriously. The family teased
him mercilessly at first, but it is clear that
he has a genuine talent for it. He has
never taken lessons, and perhaps if he did
so he would lose the naivety of style
which gives his pictures so much life. He
has a naturally good eye, with a love for
bright colours and an ability to blend
them effectively, and he has achieved
considerable success as a painter, even
...th the critics. A gallery in Milan now
has sole agency of his work, and organ-
izes exhibitions to coincide with his
engagements abroad as well as at home.

LEFT *Starting w...*
in both oils and acry...
being buildings, landscap...
scenes.
RIGHT *One of the first exhibit...*
Luciano's paintings, held in the clo...
the Basilica at Assisi.

'His pockets have been torn to shreds by the bent nails he has picked up from backstage floorboards all over the world, but he would no more go on without one than without his famous white handkerchief.'

8   Tests and Talismans

The greatest fear for an opera singer is that the voice will let you down, and when Luciano wakes up on the morning of a performance his thoughts turn instantly to the condition of his voice. He starts the day, as always, with a coffee, and then spends a minute or two on vocal exercises to check that the voice is there. If all is well, he relaxes, and if not he tries it again, pushing it steadily until it loosens up. He rarely gets up before noon, and his usual pattern is to spend the afternoon quietly, concentrating his thoughts on the evening ahead, painting, doing crossword puzzles and watching television, often entirely alone. His telephone calls are screened by his secretary and he sleeps as much as he can. Days when he is not performing are frequently filled with rehearsals, interviews, recording sessions and meetings, but he would be quite incapable of working for eight hours at a stretch, as other people do, and long periods of rest and relaxation are vital to him.

Luciano has always had a huge capacity for sleep. When he was young he could sleep for twelve or fifteen hours at a stretch, and although his need for it has diminished a little he is always the first in the family to go to bed and sleeps a lot more than most people do. Naturally the voice tends to be in good form and *piena di sole* – full of sunshine – when he is rested. Then he can use its full range of colour and tone, playing it like the subtlest of instruments rather than simply concentrating on producing the notes, as he has to do if it is out of condition.

Before a performance he is either very tense or very calm – there is never a middle course with Luciano – and

In thoughtful mood whilst on a tour of the Soviet Union to raise funds for a hospital in Armenia after the earthquake of 1988.

although his calmness is often the result of confidence in the state of his voice, the need to ask more of himself when he is tense and anticipating certain disaster has been known to produce spectacular results. The higher you climb the more is expected of you, and he regards every night as a test in which he has to prove himself. If you are known by everyone and you give a bad performance *that* will be known by everyone too, but his expectations of himself are an even bigger spur to do well and they fuel the tension more than anything. If the public are ever disappointed in him he is sure to be infinitely more disappointed in himself for failing to achieve his own high standards.

He is always surrounded by a retinue of 'runners', and in the hours and minutes before he goes on stage life can become quite tiring for those in attendance. He is not what you might call a patient man, but his bursts of irritation evaporate the minute his demands are met. His secretary becomes adept at knowing when to leave him in peace in his dressing room and when to hover in case of immediate need; in an opera house there are dressers to see to his costume, but before a concert it is she who checks that his white tie and tails are in order, helps him with his make-up, sees that ample quantities of iced water and fresh lemons have been provided in his dressing room and that every potential catastrophe has been safely averted.

There is a certain well-known ritual that must always be observed before Luciano goes on stage, and it has brought about the ruination of nearly all his trousers. His pockets have been torn to shreds by the bent nails he has picked up from backstage floorboards all over the world, but he would no more go on without one than without his famous white handkerchief. In Italy we touch metal rather than wood for good luck and horns are said to ward off evil spirits,

ABOVE *Luciano is not a moody man but the tensions of his working life are considerable and have to be confronted every time he performs.*
OPPOSITE *In rehearsal for a recital in Central Park, New York, June 1991.*

so a bent nail neatly combines two talismans in one. He has been sent them in their hundreds – big ones, little ones, silver ones, even solid gold ones – but nothing is a substitute for finding one himself. He always succeeds because someone always ensures that he does. Luciano knows that more often than not the bent nail that he finds en route from his dressing room to the stage has been 'planted' for his benefit, but the conspiracy is all part of the ritual. He says he first used the white handkerchief to discourage himself from throwing his arms around too wildly – as we Italians are apt to do – but like Linus's blanket in the Peanuts cartoon it gives him a sense of security, and, once having adopted it,

to give it up would be tempting fate.

He will always follow the same route to a particular destination, and almost invariably stays in the same hotels, not just because it is pleasanter to be on familiar territory but because to change might bring bad luck. Practically everyone in the theatre seems to be a little superstitious, but Luciano is more so than most. He is genuinely annoyed if the salt is passed from hand to hand without being put down on the table in between, and will never travel on Friday the 17th (the equivalent for Italians of Friday the 13th) if he can possibly avoid it; it is a day to lie low and take no chances.

He has a fear, unconnected with superstition but nevertheless irrational, that he

Although he is frequently teased for employing such a theatrical prop, the white handkerchief has become both a talisman and a trademark for Luciano and he never performs in concert without it.

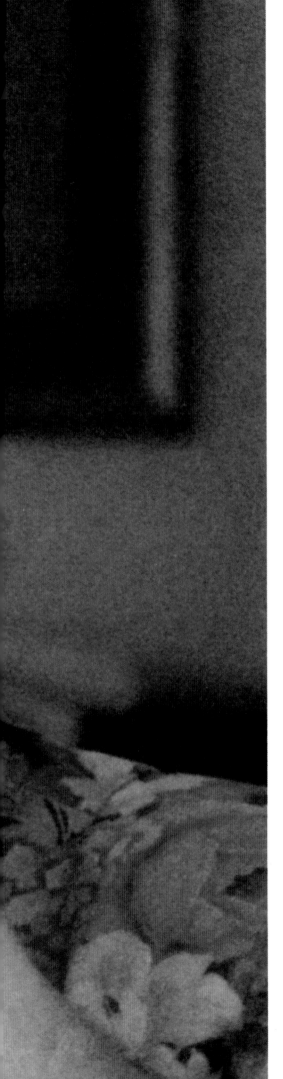

For operatic roles Luciano relies on the skills of professional make-up artists, but any running repairs required in the interval he carries out himself.

will be stuck in a lift and die of suffocation. Once, when we were staying at the Hotel Fenice in Venice, the lift did stop for a second or two and, although there was no real cause for alarm, Luciano immediately broke into a sweat and began shouting for help. On another occasion we were on our way to dinner in London with our friend Enid Blech when again the lift momentarily stopped; Luciano shook the doors so violently I was afraid he would smash them to pieces and we would really be stuck. Everything has to be big – hotel rooms, clothes, everything – not simply to accommodate him but because he hates to feel trapped.

This dislike of confined spaces also extends to aeroplanes, but his fear of flying is understandable because on 22 December 1975 he was involved in a plane crash which could easily have cost him his life. He was coming home for Christmas from America and, since all

Alitalia planes to and from northern Italy had been grounded by the usual winter fog in the Lombardy Plain, he was booked on to a TWA flight from New York to Malpensa, Milan. Everything was fine until they approached Malpensa Airport. The fog was dense, and in order to assess landing conditions the pilot took the plane down low, hovering at a 45° angle and swerving up again sharply when the ground was in sight. This manoeuvre caused general alarm among the passengers, and, when he announced that he would fly on to Geneva if the weather showed no signs of improving, Luciano cried out 'Do it!'. However a few minutes later the pilot made up his mind to try again. They went down in another steep descent and it seemed they had landed safely, but the plane was still moving at high speed when it careered off the runway. The right wing tilted and broke off at the tip, cutting loose its two jet engines, and as the severed wing hit

the ground the plane was thrown up in the air, twisted, and came to land again with such force that the fuselage split in two. In front of Luciano's seat was a gaping hole where the first class cabin had been. Incredibly, it turned out that no one had been killed and only a few slightly injured, and everyone managed to struggle out of the emergency exits and slide to the ground. Then they ran for their lives: they could smell fuel and feared that at any moment the plane might go up in flames. Eventually a series of buses loomed up through the freezing fog and ferried passengers to the terminal, where Luciano rang me. He was anxious that I should hear the news of the crash from him before seeing it on the television. His dear friend Franco Casarini had gone to Malpensa to meet him and, while other flights were announced as having been diverted to Venice, Trieste or Geneva, there was no information on Luciano's. Finally word filtered through that there had been an accident, but radio contact with the plane had been lost and for at least an hour no further details were supplied. Naturally Franco feared that an accident meant fatalities, and I think that hour of waiting was the longest of his life. When the pair of them arrived home not long before dawn it was clear that the crash had shaken Luciano badly, and he had nightmares about it for a year or two afterwards. It brought home to us all very forcefully the importance of his life. Unusually for him, he had been depressed for a while before it happened, and has often said that it renewed his spirit of optimism and made him see that he had a huge amount to live for.

Affectionately greeting his closest friend, Franco Casarini. Franco was touched that Luciano had hired a plane to travel back from a concert engagement in Frankfurt to attend the wedding of his daughter Adriana in Correggio, near Modena.

He had no choice but to continue to fly – his career depends upon it – and one might imagine that travelling as much as he does would be stressful in itself. In fact he survives it very well. Sometimes when he is on tour he rings me and says 'We're packing the suitcases now', and I know very well that he hasn't been near the suitcases, and that it is his secretary who is feverishly gathering together all his possessions, packing costumes, wigs and music, checking off passport, documents and tickets, just as I do when I travel with him. He has of course to conserve his energies, and the only requirement of him usually is to move from the apartment to the waiting car and from there to the aeroplane. Sometimes he travels on to another city the day after a performance, rehearses, sings and leaves again without seeing any more than airports, hotels and concert halls, but the frequent changes do not seem to bother him, and the fact that he is mostly indoors means that climatic differences affect him very little. If I am about to fly out and join him and need to know what clothes to take, he invariably says 'Bring a gaberdine'; according to him, all problems of what to wear are solved by a gaberdine.

If he goes out in cold weather he muffles his face and neck with scarves to protect himself from throat infections, which singers dread more than anything. When they do get ill, cancelling an engagement is always the last resort: not only does their reputation for professionalism depend on their reliability but they also let the audience down and lose their fee. Yet the public seems reluctant sometimes to take a singer's ailments seriously. In 1983 Luciano was forced to cancel five performances of *Tosca* at Covent Garden because at the last minute he was ill, and he was criticized quite severely for it in the English press. Whether it was the conviction that all opera singers are subject to tantrums and tears, or the British habit of saying they

are fine when they are clearly at death's door that persuaded them he was malingering, we shall never know, but after that he kept away from Britain for a while for fear of another rebuff. The rift did not last, however, and he very happily does an opera at Covent Garden nearly every season now.

In matters of health, as in all things, Luciano's habits are extravagant, and he regulates the state of his body from minute to minute with pills of every conceivable kind – vitamins, nature cures

and homeopathic remedies in addition to conventional medicines: pills for digestion, for indigestion, for the liver, the heart and the kidneys, to keep him awake, to send him to sleep, pills as prophylactics as well as to treat suspected complaints, and he checks his blood pressure (and that of anyone nearby) at regular intervals throughout the day if he feels at all unwell. He very rarely goes to the doctor, but if he does so he goes armed with his own detailed diagnosis and, not content with that, has even been

known to carry out an examination of the doctor.

Luciano is not immune, especially if he has had too much to eat the night before, from feeling a little fragile in the morning, but he has few ailments other than the ones we are all occasionally subject to. He does, however, suffer a good deal of pain as a result of an accident playing football at the age of twelve, when he fell on a nail which set up a septicaemic infection in his leg. This was in 1947; penicillin was just beginning

ABOVE *Protecting his throat from the cold in Leningrad, May 1990.*
LEFT AND BELOW *A grim-faced Luciano muffled up to the ears in Chicago and London, 1991.*

to be made available to civilians in Italy and Luciano was one of the first to be treated with it. The infection did not respond immediately and he was so near to death that a priest was sent for to administer the last rites, but gradually the fever subsided and he pulled through. Had it not been for the penicillin the doctors would have had to amputate the leg in order to save his life. Instead they removed the infected part of the hip joint, and he was told that in his late forties he would be likely to have trouble in walking. They were right, but we hope the hip socket will be replaced before long and that that will solve the problem.

In spite of his love of sport, Luciano finds it no hardship to lead a sedentary life. He is really very happy to be waited on, which unfortunately reduces his incentive to slim. He began to get heavy soon after he started his singing career, when he no longer needed big meals to feed his energy but could not break the eating habits he had developed as a boy. At the age of forty he went on his first major diet and lost nearly 80 lb. (36 kg.), but he always gains what he loses, and usually a bit extra besides. He would love to be thinner, but he loves his food even more, especially pasta and rice, and that makes it very hard to sustain the necessary effort. It is not a simple issue in any case. His size has undoubtedly helped to make him famous, but being overweight brings with it endless problems affecting his career as well as his personal life. It inevitably precludes him from playing certain roles in full-costume stage productions, and past experience does not suggest that his voice would be affected by a substantial loss of weight (though this argument is frequently used in defence of maintaining the status quo). He is far more concerned about his appearance than people may imagine and hates to be photographed from unflattering angles. On the other hand, even if the tensions of his working day do not account

for his appetite, eating does help him to relax. It is also true that both Luciano and his father feel weak unless they are well padded, though there is a limit and, while Fernando manages to stay within it, Luciano somehow doesn't. He is full of good intentions, and assurances that this time the diet will last, but his love of food invariably gets the upper hand.

Never a man to compromise, when he commits himelf to a diet the entire household is dominated by the new regime and everybody becomes a martyr to the cause. Special ingredients have to be hunted down in special shops, weighed and mixed with special utensils and stored in special containers, and

Luciano consumes quantities of iced mineral water with fresh lemon juice, both as a substitute for food and in order to lubricate the throat.

when he travels two extra suitcases – one for utensils, scales and containers, another for the food itself – have to accompany him around the world. He has tried a range of dietary concoctions over the years, and finds the best for him is a mixture of chicken and cooked vegetables, with a small amount of pasta or rice; it can be prepared in advance, stored in a fridge and eaten cold, which avoids the hazards of the cooking and waiting period, when he is tempted to pick at other food. He knows the calorific value of every item, and what tricks to use to cheat his appetite into thinking it is satisfied, but he is still a better advertisement for Italian food than he is for any diet. After all, it is one of his greatest pleasures in life.

*'He has never been
slow to take up a challenge
within the scope of
his own capabilities,
believing as a general principle
that the greater the risk
the richer the rewards.'*

9   *The Business of Singing*

Almost overnight, after Luciano's first great triumph at the Met in 1972 with *La Fille du Régiment*, he was in demand for newspaper interviews and television talk shows all over the United States, and this publicity in its turn brought him many more offers of work. He needed someone to advise him on which to accept and which refuse, someone who could deal with opera house and concert hall managements, who could handle the media, negotiate his fees and recording contracts and schedule his engagements worldwide. Up to this point he had had agents representing him in a number of different countries but never an international manager with whom they could all liaise.

Since 1968 an American agent, Herbert Breslin, had handled Luciano's publicity in the United States, as he did for other artists, but in 1972 he became his manager. Herbert's network of contacts

and knowledge of the workings of both the opera world and the media made him an ideal person to help Luciano explore his full potential, and they were two of a kind in being energetic and adventurous but at the same time realistic, practical and highly professional. From the very beginning they formed a partnership of such mutual trust and confidence that in twenty years there has never been a formal contract between them; they have an unwritten understanding and feel no need of anything more.

It was clear to Herbert Breslin at once that in terms of publicity Luciano's personality was almost as big an asset as his voice, and that merely presenting him

The late American conductor and composer Leonard Bernstein discussing a point of interpretation with Luciano during a concert rehearsal at the Avery Fisher Hall, New York, 8 November 1987.

to the right audiences at the right time would make him into an international star. It would also enable Luciano to achieve his aim of extending opera to a wider public. It was Herbert who encouraged him to do solo concerts and organized his first major recital at Carnegie Hall, New York, in 1973. In some respects this was a gamble because it was a highly prestigious venue and a failure could have been as conspicuous as a success; Herbert's unshakeable confidence in the venture was not at the outset shared in equal measure by Luciano. Very few opera singers have what it takes to fill a concert hall and to keep an audience enthralled with a programme of twenty arias and songs in different styles without the backing of a full operatic

production, and in spite of his triumph at the Met Luciano was still fairly inexperienced to take on New York single-handed. As a trial run he gave concerts in Liberty, Missouri, and Dallas, Texas, and his successes there convinced him that he could do it and that the likely dividends made the risk worth taking. The fees are far higher for a solo recital than for an operatic performance, and the audience, especially if the event is broadcast and recorded, is potentially vast. His triumph at Carnegie Hall was sensational, and his televised concert from the Met in 1978, an even bigger challenge, was said to have had twelve million viewers.

In the United States particularly, perhaps, promotion plays a vital part in a

performer's success, and Herbert Breslin's instinctively sound judgement on how to use it to the best advantage helped in the early days to establish Luciano in the eyes of the public. He arranged appearances on the Johnny Carson Show, negotiated *Time* and *Newsweek* cover stories and Luciano's only venture into advertising, a commercial for American Express. In 1980 he was instrumental in organizing a concert performance of *Rigoletto* in Central Park, New York, with Luciano playing the Duke, which had an audience of two hundred thousand people.

All the requests for concert and opera bookings, television appearances and interviews that are filtered through agents in other countries are coordinated by

ABOVE LEFT *Luciano with members of the team who help organize his working life: his manager, Herbert Breslin (seated left); Tibor Rudas, who handles his arena concerts (standing left); and London impresario Harvey Goldsmith (standing right).*

ABOVE *A pat on the head for Herbert Breslin during the interval of a concert in the Roman amphitheatre at Orange in the South of France, 1989.*

RIGHT *Luciano likes to make himself accessible to everyone and is happy to give interviews whenever his schedule permits: at a press conference at the Dorchester Hotel, London, November 1991.*

OVERLEAF *With a television crew in the garden of our house in Modena, 1991.*

Herbert Breslin in liaison with Stage Door Opera Management, which I run from offices at our house in Modena, and Luciano then decides which ones to take up, planning his future schedules as much as four or five years ahead. Since 1986 the organization and promotion of his arena concerts worldwide has been handled by Tibor Rudas, a Hungarian agent based in New York, who works closely with both Herbert and Stage Door. I arrange Luciano's now infrequent engagements in Italy, among the most recent being the televised concert on 29 April 1991 in Reggio Emilia to mark the anniversary of his début there in *La Bohème*, the prize for the Achille Peri competition which he had won exactly thirty years before.

I started the agency in 1987. As a result of living and travelling with Luciano I had acquired a certain knowledge of the opera business and was frequently asked by young singers for help in getting a foot on the ladder. In an unofficial capacity at first, I approached the conductors, casting directors and opera house managers whom I knew, learned who was looking for singers for forthcoming productions and whenever possible arranged auditions. The next task was to negotiate a contract on behalf of the singer, and then to arrange further introductions and represent them in any subsequent engagements. Before long I found myself involved in every aspect of their career and personally committed to its promotion. Apart from contacts, and a degree of knowledge and taste, I believe integrity and common sense are the principal qualities required of an agent, together with an ability to identify with the average audience, which more often than not is discouraged by an uncompromisingly intellectual approach.

I never expected Stage Door to become as successful or as time-consuming as it has done, but it goes against the grain to do anything half-heartedly and I have given myself to it body and soul. A twelve-hour working day and constant travelling have somehow to be fitted around the other priorities of my life – which naturally centre on the family and on the houses at Modena and Pesaro – while ensuring that nothing vital is neglected and that Luciano's periods at home are as restful as it is possible to make them.

The opportunity to see the very finest productions all over the world has given me an increasing sense of commitment to opera and a reluctance to accept anything less than the best, and I love being part of this very Italian tradition and helping it

to thrive. Some of the young singers I represent have been with me since I started the business and are now well established, and I take an almost maternal interest in their progress. There is great excitement and gratification to be derived from giving them the opportunities they deserve.

Faxes fly between Stage Door and Herbert Breslin's New York office every day of the week with up-dates on developments in the Pavarotti programme. Luciano is now the centre of a symbiotic group of promotion executives, accountants, agents, public relations officers, assistants and secretaries, caught up in a

BELOW LEFT *Luciano has worked exclusively with Decca Records throughout his career; in discussion with Maestro Zubin Mehta and Antonella Banaudi during a new recording of* Il Trovatore, *1991.*
BELOW *My own working life keeps me involved in every aspect of Luciano's itinerary.*

> *With every new recording Luciano endeavours to extend his knowledge of the music he sings and to bring something fresh to its interpretation.*

whirl of business meetings and computerized itineraries. Competition and big investment in the performing arts calls for a more rigorous approach than in the past, and, although it may be a good thing that this has virtually eliminated the old-style prima donna from the opera circuit, it can also turn singers, whose voices are inseparable from their identities, into rather colourless performers. Every working week for years ahead is pre-programmed and they live their lives in aeroplanes and limousines, moving between anonymous hotel suites and featureless concert halls – hardly an existence calculated to encourage high spirits and spontaneity. The fact that Luciano is irrepressible by nature and that his personality survives all this unscathed makes him an even more unusual phenomenon in an increasingly sober world. It has helped him to resist the dehumanizing process, as has his desire to please: ever since he was a little boy giving concerts for the neighbours he has liked to entertain people and gratify their wishes, and this persuades him to accede whenever possible to requests for interviews and press conferences, which help to sustain the individuality of his public image.

ABOVE AND LEFT *Working on a recording of* Rigoletto *with conductor Riccardo Chailly and members of a Decca crew in Bologna, July 1989.*

When work is in short supply there is a natural temptation to accept every offer that comes your way, but Luciano has always been aware of the need to pace himself in order to safeguard his voice. Even in the early days, when he desperately wanted a contract from La Scala, he turned down their offer of the lead in Rossini's *Guillaume Tell* because he knew that the role was too heavy for him and that if he took it it would ruin his voice. Equally, he has never been slow to take up a challenge within the scope of his own capabilities, believing as a general principle that the greater the risk the richer the rewards, although he is prepared to admit that some ventures have proved less successful than others. The film *Yes, Giorgio*, made in Hollywood by MGM in 1982, was not his greatest triumph, but he thoroughly enjoyed his part in it, and found the film-making process stimulating because it required him to adapt to working methods quite different from those he was used to. Initial discussions between the director, Franklin J. Schaffner (best known for *Papillon* and *Nicholas and Alexandra*), the English producer, Peter Fetterman, and other members of the cast were complex and protracted, and after one meeting, held in Modena, Luciano decided that they all deserved a taste of some of the best food Emilia Romagna can provide. He took them to Fini's, an old and very famous *modenese* restaurant, where the meal was so delicious and everyone became so relaxed and well disposed towards the owner that it was agreed the hero of the film, an Italian tenor played by Luciano, should be called after him, Giorgio Fini. The film took thirteen weeks to make and cost $21,000,000, but it was criticized for its sentimentality and for being out of step with the 1980s – one of its saving graces in Luciano's opinion – and it was not a commercial success.

Now that I travel less with Luciano than in the past I am spared the round of

grand celebrity receptions that he is expected to attend, but it is always exciting to meet people who have climbed to the top of their particular tree. The party given by MGM to launch *Yes, Giorgio* was a line-up of the great and glamorous of the American cinema – Cary Grant, Gregory Peck, Rod Steiger, Burt Lancaster, Charlton Heston, Angie Dickinson, Kirk Douglas – and it was a particular thrill for Luciano because he loves the movies of the great age of

Hollywood and remembers the names of all the stars from his childhood.

He has always had a curiosity about life and people, and one of the bonuses of branching out into new areas of work is meeting stars across a wider spectrum – giving recitals with singers such as Diana Ross and Frank Sinatra for example – never in order to compete in their field of entertainment but always in the hope of bringing back a few more converts to his own.

OPPOSITE ABOVE AND BELOW *In MGM's Yes, Giorgio, made in 1982, Luciano was typecast as an extrovert Italian tenor who enjoys his food and leaves chaos behind him in the kitchen.*

ABOVE *Family reaction to the film: Giuliana (left), Cristina and I (right), flanking Luciano at the Italian premiere in Modena.*

In 1983 he made his second film, which was a very different experience from the first. The great French director Jean-Pierre Ponnelle, with whom Luciano had worked a number of times on the stage, offered him the role of the Duke of Mantua in a film version of *Rigoletto*. Ponnelle, who sadly died in 1988 at the age of fifty-six, had a wonderful ability to visualize an ensemble in its entirety and give it movement, and Luciano had great admiration for his work. Since the opera

is set in and around Mantua and much of the action takes place at night, a large part of the location work was shot close to where we live, and many nocturnal hours were spent waiting instead of sleeping while tiny fragments of scenes were put together. It was exhausting but for Luciano it was also exciting and rewarding; under Ponnelle's direction he interpreted the role of the libertine Duke with heightened intensity and gave a great performance.

He has been asked to do innumerable films over the last ten years and would like to do more, especially adaptations of opera in order to disseminate it more widely. The problem is time. If he agrees to do a film it means committing himself to several months away from the opera and concert stages, a sacrifice that he would be prepared to make only for an offer that was truly irresistible. It may come.

We have made some wonderful friends in the film world. Until he died in March 1987 we used to see Danny Kaye whenever we went to New York and loved him dearly. Not only was he an authority on the subject of opera but he also shared Luciano's passion for cooking, and they would have regular discussions over breakfast about Maria Callas's interpretation of *Tosca* or where to buy the best ingredients for a bouillabaisse. He was a sweet and delightful person, unaffected and genuine, and he never had his head turned by his own publicity. Luciano is well aware

that as a celebrity himself he is surrounded by hangers-on, but people mean too much to him to be cynical about their motives; as he says, you can finish up distrusting everyone and have no friends at all. Famous people are almost invariably held in awe by the public, which gives relationships with them an awkwardness and artificiality that can be hard to overcome, but the rare talents that raise certain people above the general run seem often to be accompanied by a simplicity and generosity of spirit that makes friendship with them especially enriching.

Luciano frequently appears before royalty or heads of state when he makes a foreign tour, and Britain's Queen Elizabeth, the Queen Mother, whom he has met on several occasions, has always charmed him with her ease of manner. Over the years he has sung for Queen Elizabeth II, the Prince and Princess of Wales, Prince Rainier of Monaco, King Juan Carlos and Queen Sophia of Spain, the late King Olaf of Norway, Presidents

Danny Kaye and I, New York, March 1976. Like many other people around the world, we lost a dear friend when he died in 1987.

Carter and Reagan, President Gorbachev, President Giscard d'Estaing, the General Secretary of the Chinese Communist Party and Pope John Paul II.

Since 1965, when Modena presented him with the Principessa Carlotta prize for his contribution to the arts, Luciano has received over 350 achievement awards – gold and silver medals, diplomas, doctorates and the keys of foreign cities; he has left his hand print in the hall of fame in Fort Lauderdale, Miami, and his waxwork stands in Madame Tussaud's; he has had critical accolades comparing him with Caruso and financial rewards greater than those of any opera singer in history. He loves it all, but he has never in his life let it create a distance between himself and other people or felt that it made him in any way superior. It may have been difficult sometimes to make the transition to a lifestyle quite different from anything we envisaged, but we have a deep sense of gratitude for the fact that so far Luciano has had no reversals in his fortune.

ABOVE *At a ceremony on 19 October 1987 in Washington DC Luciano and Sophia Loren were two of the recipients of the Christopher Columbus award for their contributions to the performing arts.*

LEFT *Though he is not a regularly practising catholic, Luciano's religious beliefs are deep and unwavering, and it meant a lot to him to be granted an audience with Pope John Paul II: on 20 June 1986 he visited the Vatican in company with the orchestra and chorus of the Teatro Margherita in Genoa for the blessing of their trip to China.*

TOP LEFT *Luciano's first award, the Principessa Carlotta Prize, presented to him in 1965 by his home town of Modena.*

TOP RIGHT *At a celebration dinner in Milan on 26 March 1980 he was awarded the Premio Agrodolce by the Italian Press Association for his contribution to opera.*

ABOVE LEFT *Luciano and Joan Sutherland at a ceremony in London, 18 November 1991, at which Luciano was nominated Artist of the Year and Joan was presented with a Lifetime Achievement Award by* Gramophone *magazine.*

ABOVE RIGHT *A tree-planting ceremony in Hyde Park, London, on 29 July 1991 to inaugurate the Prince of Wales's Tree Appeal; £100,000 was donated to the fund from the sale of television and recording rights in Luciano's open-air concert, which took place the following day.*

On holiday at Pesaro in 1989 Luciano was measured up in his concert tail coat for a waxwork at Madame Tussaud's, where his double now stands; he is the only opera singer in history to appear there.

*'He wants to pass on to
a new generation of singers
the operatic inheritance that
he received when he came
into this world, and if he is
popularizing opera in the process then he is achieving what
he set out to do and nothing could make him happier.'*

10 Opera for the Future

One of the benefits of his success that Luciano most enjoys is freedom of choice. He has earned the luxury of being able to choose what he does, and even occasionally of initiating new projects in which he would like to be involved. His years of experience have not only given him a deeper understanding of the music he sings and a more profound pleasure in it but also allow him greater participation in the overall interpretation of any work he undertakes, which is in itself an immense source of satisfaction. Interpretation is obviously subjective, and when different musicians are striving after incompatible ideals it can sometimes lead to conflict, but as Joan Sutherland has said, 'You can always work it out with Luciano'. If he takes a stand on the way a particular phrase is played or sung it is only ever in the interests of perfection; he hates indifference and it upsets him to see things done in a way that fails to meet his own exacting standards.

Top international singers are made to feel a certain obligation to perform all the major roles within their range at some point in their career, as if, like Hercules, only by completing their allotted labours can they hope to achieve immortality. With the criteria Luciano is determined to satisfy, especially at this stage in his career, adding a new role to his repertoire can require two to three years of study,

Elisabeth Holloque with Luciano in a production of Tosca *at the Pittsburgh Opera House, Philadelphia, May 1989.*

but he has always taken pleasure in giving the public what they want and also in widening his own horizons.

In December 1988 he tried out his talents as a director, assisted by our daughter Cristina, with a production of Donizetti's *La Favorita* at the famous La Fenice theatre in Venice. It was a great success, and he found it exhilarating to make an opera come together piece by piece under his own direction. Since then he has been invited to work as a director with a number of other companies, but so far he has been too fully occupied with long-standing engagements to repeat the experiment.

It is only recently that Luciano has felt inclined to take up the challenge of a role that for any tenor is one of the most testing: *Otello*. An intensely dramatic part, it is almost baritone in its colouration, and Luciano's voice, with its limpid clarity and pure upper register, has always been more suited to the lyrical, romantic tenor leads. Because he has

paced himself carefully over the years his voice has lost none of its top notes and its distinctive quality has never changed, but, as always happens as a singer grows older, it has acquired a slightly darker natural colour, bringing some of the heavier tenor roles within his range. *Otello* was Georg Solti's swansong with the Chicago Symphony Orchestra, where he had been resident conductor since 1969, and accepting his offer of the part was Luciano's way of paying homage to a great maestro. The opera was performed in a concert form with Kiri te Kanawa as Desdemona and Leo Nucci as Iago.

Chicago, with its vicious winds and intense cold, seems to be jinxed for Luciano – an infection almost invariably grabs him by the throat the minute he arrives – and this time he was attacked by a flu virus before opening night which sadly prevented him from giving of his best. It also struck down Solti himself (who conducted the first performance with a temperature of 101) and half the

FAR LEFT *With Leo Nucci, Sir Georg Solti and Dame Kiri te Kanawa at a rehearsal of Verdi's* Otello *in Chicago, April 1991.*
LEFT AND ABOVE *Maestro Sir Georg Solti was taking his leave of the Chicago Symphony Orchestra after twenty-two years.*

ABOVE *Leo Nucci as Iago, Dame Kiri te Kanawa as Desdemona and Luciano as Otello at the end of the first performance in Chicago. Making his début in the title role, Luciano felt as though he was wrestling with one of the great dragons of the operatic stage.*

LEFT *Luciano has performed Canio's famous aria 'Vesti la giubba' from Leoncavallo's* I Pagliacci *many times, and in 1981 he appeared in costume to do so for a television programme entitled 'Pavarotti and Friends'. He will undertake the role for the first time in a full stage production, following concert performances in Philadelphia and New York, at La Scala in 1993.*

orchestra too. In spite of this the audience reception was overwhelmingly appreciative, and the opera critic Andrew Porter, writing in the *New Yorker,* said of Luciano: 'His voice sounded the music with a thrilling clarity and firmness of word and tone ... in Othello's blazing monologues he was brilliant.'

Making his début as Canio, Luciano appeared in a concert version of Leoncavallo's *I Pagliacci,* conducted by Riccardo Muti (and recorded in 1991), in Philadelphia on 5 February 1992, with further performances in New York the following week. This is to be followed by a full costume production at La Scala in 1993. It means a lot to Luciano to take on a role for which one of his greatest heroes, Caruso, was famous, and it strengthens his sense of belonging to a continuing tradition of Italian tenors, but it also heightens all the usual anxieties inherent in undertaking new work. It would not be normal or even advantageous to be free of such doubts, but so far I believe – and have been reassuring him throughout our married life – he has always produced something in a class of its own.

As well as expanding his repertoire Luciano continues to perform many of the roles for which he has been famous throughout his career, and aims to polish and refine them with every production. This constant process of renewal is vital

to him, and the satisfaction and fulfilment he derives from the music he sings shines out of his face now more than ever. One result of his success is the opportunity it gives him to share with other people the advantages that life has given him, and benefit concerts are a practical means of doing this. Being a good Italian, the causes closest to his heart are those which have affected the family: research into *myasthenia gravis,* a rare muscular condition which our youngest daughter, Giuliana, contracted (and recovered from, thanks to Ameri-

TOP LEFT *At Radio City Music Hall with Frank Sinatra, 24 January 1982, in a concert to raise money for the Sloan Kettering Memorial Hospital, New York.*
TOP RIGHT *Luciano arriving with his parents at a dinner after a fund-raising recital in Modena, 5 May 1987. His mother's fear of being overcome by emotion if she were to see him in a live performance confines her to watching him only on television.*
ABOVE *Luciano and I at a benefit evening held on 20 October 1988 at the Cinema Raffaello, Modena, in aid of handicapped children.*

Teaching has become an increasing source of fulfilment for Luciano. At the Juilliard School in New York's Lincoln Center in 1979 he gave his first series of masterclasses.

can expertise) at the age of sixteen; leukaemia, from which his sister Gabriella's three-year-old daughter died; and muscular dystrophy, which keeps his nephew Luca, his sister's other child, permanently confined to a wheelchair. Aside from such personal concerns, the causes he supports are multifarious: in San Francisco and Chicago in 1981 he took part in concerts in aid of victims of the Naples earthquake disaster; in January 1982 and again in March 1984 he appeared in concert with Frank Sinatra at New York's Radio City Music Hall, where they raised a million dollars for cancer research at the Sloan Kettering Memorial Hospital; at a series of benefit concerts in Oklahoma in 1983 enough money was raised to fund the building of a new wing for a local hospital; and he helps to maintain the Casa Verdi, a home for retired opera singers in Milan. He also demonstrates his tacit support for certain political causes: he decided long ago never to perform in South Africa while apartheid was government policy, particularly in view of the fact that all the pressing invitations to do so came from people who had no wish to change the regime.

One of his keenest ambitions is to help young singers to make the most of their talents, and he has proved himself to be an excellent teacher, tirelessly patient in the interests of perfection. He can often identify very precisely what is missing in the rendition of a piece and enable students to transform their interpretation into something expressive and beautiful. Young singers seek him out wherever he is – at home, at hotels where he is staying on tour, and at opera houses all over the world – and only if circumstances leave him no choice does he refuse a request for help, frequently

Working on the score of Aida *(with the conductor Lorin Maazel), which was to open the 1985 season of La Scala.*

It has been said that Luciano can reach out through his voice to the hearts and minds of people, and that by virtue of his natural appeal and ability to communicate he is uniquely equipped to promote the future of opera.

taking students to a theatre in order to hear them sing in the right surroundings. He has given several very successful series of masterclasses at the Juilliard School in New York, and looks forward to the day when there is more time in his life for teaching so that he can do everything possible to pass on to young singers the lessons he has learned himself.

One of the principal ways in which he helps to foster their development is through the Opera Company of Philadelphia's biennial International Voice Competition, which began in 1981 when Luciano was celebrating the twentieth anniversary of the launch of his career. The Philadelphia Opera House asked him how they could most fittingly recognize his long association with them, and he said that, more than anything, he would like a singing competition to be established in his name. Philadelphia is a rich city, full of wealthy families willing to patronize the arts, and the sponsorship needed to fund the competition has been generously provided. Luciano gives his services free and it takes up a good deal of his time, but he derives enormous gratification from his involvement in it. Around three thousand young singers compete internationally and, while two adjudicators carry out a selection process around the world, Luciano judges heats held in Pesaro, Modena and New York, and in other cities where they can be arranged to coincide with his singing engagements. The following year he

Young contestants in the European finals and world semi-finals of the Philadelphia International Voice Competition, at the Teatro Comunale, Modena, 8 January 1985.

judges the world final, which is held in Philadelphia. The opera in which the winners take part has to be something from Luciano's own repertoire because in order to attract the public and the necessary publicity he takes the tenor lead. No diploma is worth very much if you never set foot on an opera stage, and the Philadelphia Competition offers students today, just as the Achille Peri prize did for Luciano in 1961, a chance to appear before an audience.

He feels a clear responsibility to give

the young as much help as he can in fulfilling their own potential and in promoting the survival of opera. To this end he hopes in the not too distant future, together perhaps with friends and colleagues, to establish a music study centre at Modena, equipped with sports and leisure facilities, where students can be offered ideal conditions for learning.

No one could give so much to music unless it meant more to them than anything else in life, and if Luciano had wished above all to lead a peaceful and

The soprano Nuccia Focile, now well established on the opera circuit, was an early winner of the Philadelphia Competition. She has sung with Luciano several times in recent years, and during his tour of Argentina they appeared together in La Bohème; *they were dancing after a performance in Buenos Aires, August 1987.*

private existence he would have had to sacrifice any idea of achieving great heights as an artist. To be married to him has given my life a value that it might not otherwise have had, but if I have a regret it is that our separate commitments keep us apart for too much of the year. One day, before we are too old to enjoy it, maybe we shall succeed in combining our lives and our work at Modena, and be free to devote time to each other as well as to music. A study centre might be the perfect means of doing so.

At a dinner held in his honour on 30 January 1988 Luciano
was presented with a Lifetime Achievement Award
by the National Italian-American Foundation,
Washington DC.

Meanwhile Luciano's dream – and mine too – would be to find, perhaps through the Philadelphia Competition or Stage Door, a young tenor who has all the essential qualities required to build a big career. Luciano will continue to sing professionally for as long as he can satisfy his own demands, but perhaps it is natural at this point in his life to be thinking of a successor, someone to whom he can pass on the tradition handed down to him by Caruso, Gigli and di Stefano, the tenors who inspired his love of opera.

In the light of Luciano's own achievement it is fascinating to read some of the things that have been said in the past about Caruso, for instance by the English music critic Robert Matthew-Walker: 'The appeal of his voice was utterly exceptional, and the rapport he managed to achieve with audiences, even through the gramophone, spread far beyond the confines of the opera house to reach ordinary men and women who acknowledged in his great voice a beauty and excitement, a tenderness and expressive appeal, which have never been surpassed.' Unlike Caruso, Luciano has had modern technology on his side, and he believes firmly in applying to opera Macchiavelli's dictum that the end justifies the means: he has exploited the full potential of the mass media in a way that no classical musician, even of his own generation, has succeeded in doing, just as Caruso would have done had he been alive today. Can it really make sense to criticize him, as happened not long ago, for having the appeal of a pop star, or to say that he has debased opera by making it popular? If it is not made more popular it will die. When the grey heads in the audience are gone there will be no one, and his free concerts, arena recitals, television appearances, videos and recordings are a means of sustaining it and making it available to everyone, just as he believes it should be.

It is sometimes said that the fees paid to top-rank singers are so high that they create a financial burden for opera houses that is in itself contributing to the demise of opera. In fact the highest paid international stars actually help its survival by attracting more sponsorship from the private sector and more publicity and, of course, by selling more tickets. Luciano has been told on a number of occasions by opera house directors that his appearances have enabled them, having paid his fee, substantially to cover their costs, which they would never have done without him.

No one pretends that opera is not in many respects an anachronism, nor that it is easy to adapt it to present economic constraints, but it contains some of the most beautiful music ever written for the human voice, and its blend of drama, music and the visual arts makes it uniquely satisfying and complete. It doesn't have to be boring; it should be stimulating, exciting and moving, and by introducing audiences to it gradually through his concerts and recordings Luciano has brought people into opera houses who had never set foot in them before. He wants to pass on in a fit and flourishing state to a new generation of singers and to 'ordinary men and women' the operatic inheritance that he received when he came into this world, and if he is popularizing opera in the process then he is achieving what he set out to do and nothing could make him happier.

Luciano and I at an informal dinner at home
in Modena, 27 July 1991.

Index

Numbers in italics refer to illustration captions

ACKNOWLEDGEMENTS

The author and publisher would like to thank Francesca Barbieri, Franco Casarini, Irene Jones and Raymond McGill for all their help and advice.

The publisher would like to thank the following for their permission to reproduce the photographs used in this book:

Archivio Pavarotti pp. 8, 12, 13 above, 14 above left, 15 above, 21, 23, 24, 25, 26, 27, 28, 29, 30, 31, 32, 33, 36 right, 37 left, 37 above right, 38, 40, 41, 43, 44, 45, 50 above, 71, 85, 102, 105 below, 109 below right, 109 above left, 114, 115, 117, 127 above, 141, 142 left, 144 above right, 151 above left, 153, 155

Foto Amista pp. 35, 42 below right

Foto Richeldi Aquilino, Modena pp. 137 right, 157

Agostino Arletti, Modena pp. 150, 154

Clive Barda/Performing Arts Library pp. 9, 10, 18–19

Robert Cahen p. 91

F. Casarini (Foto Pietro Panniggiani) pp. 124–5

Foto Donia, Reggio Emilia p. 144 above left

Corrado Maria Falsini, Rome p. 17 below

Susanne Faulkner Stevens p. 152

Foto Felici, Rome p. 143 below

Enrico Ferorelli, Milan p. 109 below left

Guy Gravett p. 39

Henry Grossman, New York pp. 119, 131

Enrico Huber, Vienna p. 15 right

Michele Iannacci/International Photo News, USA pp. 143 above, 156

Winnie Klotz/Metropolitan Opera Association Inc., New York pp. 17 above, 118

Judith Kovacs pp. 1, 16, 60 above right, 61 above right, 68, 70, 90, 92, 93, 96 below, 103, 104 above left, 105 above left, 108, 109 above right, 110, 111, 112–13, 122–3, 126, 128–9, 132, 133 above, 133 below, 139 right, 144 below left, 144 below right, 145, 146, 147

Lillofoto, Palermo p. 36 left

Foto Marco, Modena pp. 13 below, 51

Robin Matthews pp. 37 below, 60 above left, 60 below left, 60 below right, 61 below, 66–7, 77, 80, 82–3, 84 left, 84 right, 101, 104 below, 105 right, 106, 116, 127 below, 134–5

Isabelle Meister/Grand Théâtre de Genève, p. 11

Foto Piccagliani pp. 42 above right, 42 below left

Patrick Piel, Hamburg p. 130

Publifoto, Milan p. 42 above left

Vivianne Purdom/The Decca Record Co. Ltd. pp. 48, 56–7, 58, 59 below, 59 above, 136, 138

Vittoriano Rastelli, Rome pp. 2, 3, 4, 14 below, 49, 52 above, 52 below, 53, 54, 55, 63, 81, 100, 120–1

Mirella Ricciardi pp. 50 below, 62, 64, 69, 72–3, 74–5, 76, 78, 79, 86–7, 88, 89, 94–5, 96 above, 97, 98–9

Jim Steere/The Decca Record Co. Ltd. pp. 148–9

M. Stradi & E. Baracchi, Modena pp. 107, 151 below, 151 above right

Reg Wilson, London pp. 46–7

Every possible effort has been made to trace and acknowledge the source of photographs and the copyright holders. The publishers sincerely apologise for any inadvertent errors or omissions and will be happy to correct them in any future edition.

British Library Cataloguing in Publication Data
A catalogue record for this book is available
from the British Library.

Designed by Harry Green
Edited by Alice Millington-Drake

Phototypeset by Keyspools Ltd, Golborne, Lancs
Colour separations by Newsele Litho Ltd
Printed and bound in Italy